CULTURES OF THE WORLD

UGANDA

Robert Barlas

MARSHALL CAVENDISH
New York • London • Sydney

Reference edition reprinted 2000 by
Marshall Cavendish Corporation
99 White Plains Road
Tarrytown
New York 10591

© Times Media Private Limited 2000

Originated and designed by
Times Books International, an imprint of
Times Media Private Limited, a member of the
Times Publishing Group

Printed in Malaysia

Library of Congress Cataloging-in-Publication Data:

Barlas, Robert.
    Uganda / Robert Barlas.
        p. cm.—(Cultures of the World)
    Includes bibliographical references (p.) and index.
    Summary: Discusses the geography, history, government,
economy, people, and culture of the African nation of Uganda.
    ISBN 0-7614-0981-5 (lib. bdg.)
    1. Uganda—Juvenile literature. [1. Uganda.] I. Title.
II. Series.
DT433.222.B37   2000
967.6—dc21   99–27577
                    CIP
                    AC

INTRODUCTION

IT HAS BEEN SAID THAT UGANDA is one of the most beautiful but complex countries in the world. It is a young country—it became independent in 1962—but is home to several of the world's oldest cultures, and to people of many ethnic origins, speaking a vast number of different languages.

Ancient tribal beliefs and customs still determine much of what takes place in Uganda today, but now the country faces the task of moving into the 21st century. Its land is fertile, the literacy rate is increasing, and the people are determined to make the country work and prosper. It is a place with much potential for the future and a rich history in its past—and somewhere more and more people from other countries want to visit to learn about the cultural background of its very varied people.

CONTENTS

A young Ugandan girl enjoys a snack on a roadside in Kampala.

CONTENTS

A vendor carries plastic containers to sell as water vessels at the market.

GEOGRAPHY

UGANDA IS SITUATED RIGHT AT THE HEART OF AFRICA. Although the country is quite small, it has a remarkably diverse landscape, ranging from the legendary snowcapped Ruwenzori Mountains to dense tropical forests, rolling plains, freshwater lakes, and breathtaking waterfalls, all inhabited by abundant wildlife.

One of the relatively few landlocked countries on the African continent, Uganda is located between the two arms of the Great Rift Valley of East Africa. The country is 93,070 square miles (241,040 sq km) in size and shares its borders with Sudan in the north, Kenya in the east, Tanzania and Rwanda in the south, and Zaire (the Democratic Republic of Congo) in the west. The western border with Zaire runs through the Western Rift Valley, which is dotted from north to south by lakes—Albert, Edward, George, and Kivu. The tropical climate supports a vast array of beautiful flora and fauna.

Opposite: **Lake Bunyoni near the Rwandan border.**

Left: **Rothschild giraffes roam near the northern border in the Kidepo National Park.**

Uganda has three subclimatic zones, differentiated mainly by altitude and rainfall. The highest levels of rainfall are around Lake Victoria. The driest regions are in the northeast and Ankole.

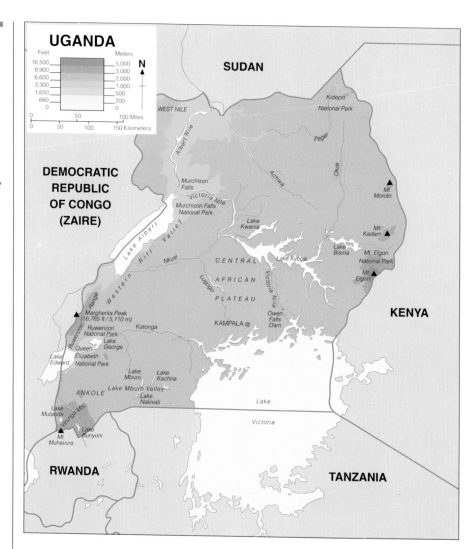

CLIMATE AND SEASONS

Overall, Uganda has what is called a modified tropical climate, which is mainly mild and pleasant. But the climate of Uganda varies a great deal throughout the country. The Equator crosses Southern Uganda, and the area is hot and sticky, with temperature variations from 60–85°F (16–30°C). The hot climate is moderated by altitude—it is cooler at the higher elevations. Rainfall also varies from region to region. Evidence of this can be seen in the changing landscape, from the dry savanna to the lush hills.

A TROPICAL PARADISE

Most of Uganda is lush and fertile, and the vegetation is extremely diverse, the result of the different climates in the country. Apart from the rather arid areas in the north, Uganda receives abundant rainfall, and about 80% of the land is fertile and suitable for agriculture. This was a major determining factor in the original settlement of the area.

The wild plants and flowers found in Uganda can be roughly classified by zones according to the amount of rainfall they receive. Much of the country's vegetation is in the flat plain-like savannas, while in the areas of high rainfall there are many trees typical of the rainforest. There is also a small area of semidesert in the north and northeast, where drought-resistant bushes, grasses, and succulent plants grow. Evergreen trees cover a large part of the country. There are rolling hills and meadows in the west and flat savannas in the east and northeast. Much of southern Uganda was formerly covered by equatorial forests, but most of these have now been cleared for human settlement.

Lush vegetation around Lake Bunyoni. It is said that Uganda is a country where the seed of any tropical fruit can germinate because of the favorable rains throughout the year.

HIGHS AND LOWS

The Ruwenzori Mountains are sometimes called the "Mountains of the Moon," due to their great height.

Much of Uganda is a plateau, with numerous small hills and valleys, and extensive savanna plains. The entire country lies in a cradle of mountains, with the volcanic Muhavura range rising over the Rift Valley.

The Ruwenzori mountains are in the west—crossing the border into Zaire and north of Lake Edward. In the center of the range, six peaks have permanent snow and glaciers. The highest of these peaks, and the third highest in Africa, is Margherita Peak, which rises to 16,765 feet (5,110 m) above sea level.

On the border with Kenya in the east towers Mount Elgon, an extinct volcano and one of the highest mountains in Africa. Because of the gradual slope, climbing to the crater rim does not require mountaineering skills. On the wooded slopes great caves, gorges, and waterfalls provide some of the most exciting scenery in Uganda, and the terraced coffee plantations and bamboo forests enhance the wonderful views.

A LAND OF LAKES

Uganda can truly be called Africa's "land of lakes," as close to 20% of the total area is covered by lakes, rivers, and waterways. The largest of these is the famous Lake Victoria, which Uganda shares with Kenya and Tanzania. This is the largest lake in Africa and the second largest body of fresh water in the world. Some of Uganda's other major lakes are Lake Edward, Lake Kwania, Lake Albert, Lake Kyoga, Lake George, and Lake Bisina. The lakes provide different attractions, such as swimming, sailing, and other water sports, and excellent fishing—Nile perch in Lake Victoria can weigh as much as 220 lbs (100 kg)!

"MOTHER" NILE

The Nile is the mightiest river in Africa and the longest in the world. Its origin is Lake Victoria and the river takes on different names as it flows through the country. From Lake Victoria it flows north to Lake Kyoga and Lake Albert as the Victoria Nile, but flowing out of Lake Albert, it joins the waters of the Albert Nile, and then enters the Sudan where it is called the White Nile.

Whitewater rapids and numerous waterfalls, such as the spectacular Murchison Falls, mark the Nile's course. Along most of its length the banks are thick with many varieties of plant life and home to water birds and the more tranquil stretches provide watering spots for the multitude of game that inhabit its shores. Giant Nile crocodiles are seen at many points along the river, either basking in the sun, or with just their eyes and noses visible as they float slowly along in the stream.

Local fishermen at the northeastern end of the Kazinga Channel near Lake George.

Above: **This site, near Jinja, is the source of the River Nile.**

Opposite: **Spectacular waterfalls are created as the Nile flows through Murchison Falls National Park north of Lake Albert.**

NATIONAL PARKS

Numerous national parks and game reserves provide a showcase for Uganda's vast array of wild animals and some of its most spectacular scenery. The parks display the extraordinary variety of the country's natural resources—freshwater lakes, swamps, mountains, forests, woodlands, rolling plains, and savanna grasslands. In order to protect and effectively manage these invaluable resources on a sustainable basis, the Uganda National Parks department was established in 1952. It presently manages 10 parks.

The Bwindi Impenetrable Forest Park occupies 120 square miles (310 sq km) in the southwest of the country on the border with Rwanda, and along with the 13-square-mile (33-sq-km) Mgahinga Gorilla Park (Uganda's smallest national park), is one of the best places to see some of the world's largest mountain gorillas—although it requires a lengthy hike to track them down!

Mount Elgon National Park is in the southeast of the country and surrounds Mount Elgon, an extinct volcano that contains a number of crater lakes. Mount Elgon is one of the best places to see the many different varieties of Ugandan birds.

In the Kibale Forest Park, chimpanzees, other monkeys, and beautiful forest birds are common. One of Uganda's most significant national parks, the Mount Ruwenzori National Park, provides some of the best, and most difficult, hiking opportunities in the country. Nearby is the Semuliki National Park, which is small but offers visitors two important attractions—refreshing hot springs and over 40 species of birds that are found nowhere else in the country.

In the northwest lies Murchison Falls National Park with its spectacular waterfalls on the Nile river. Along with the Queen Elizabeth National Park and Lake Mburo Valley in the southwest, as well as the remote Kidepo National Park in the northeast, Murchison Falls National Park provides some of the best opportunities to see big game animals in the country. These parks are all flat savanna parks with plenty of wide open spaces in which the animals roam freely.

Antelope, impala, and dik-dik are some of the animals that occupy the wide open grasslands of the Queen Elizabeth National Park.

THE ANIMAL KINGDOM

The biggest Ugandan land animals are the elephant, the rhinoceros, and the giraffe. Elephants are among the most impressive animals in the world and are present in most national parks, while the rhinoceros is among the biggest species of animals in Africa and can be very dangerous when threatened. The best place to see giraffes in Uganda is Murchison Falls National Park.

Crocodiles, one of Africa's most awesome predators, are found in Uganda. They can grow to over 20 feet (6 m) long. Although they are primarily fish eaters, they are responsible for more human deaths than any other vertebrate in Africa. Other reptiles include the rock python, one of the largest snakes in the world, and the African mamba—a venomous and aggressive snake.

Many species in the cat family can also be seen in the savannas in Uganda's national parks, including lions, leopards, wild cats, and cheetahs— one of the world's fastest animals.

UGANDAN MONKEYS

Uganda is one of the best countries in the world in which to see monkeys of different kinds living in their natural habitat. Members of the primate family found in Uganda include gorillas, chimpanzees, baboons, and velvet monkeys, as well as De'Graza and patas monkeys, many of which swing in the trees in the forests of the national parks. Ruwenzori black and white colobus (Abyssinian) monkeys are widespread in the highland forests and eat mainly leaves. The diet of other monkeys consists primarily of fruits and seeds. Gorillas can be seen near the border of Zaire and Rwanda. The area is home to the largest population of gorillas in the world.

The crested crane is Uganda's national emblem and is depicted on Uganda's flag. It lives along lakes, swamps, and grasslands, where it can be found in large flocks.

Kampala is a bustling capital city, with a mixture of low- and high-rise office buildings.

MAJOR CITIES

Kampala, the capital city of Uganda, has a population of approximately 800,000. Other major cities include Jinja (65,000), Mbale (54,000), Masaka (50,000), Entebbe (43,000), Mbarara (41,000), and Gulu (38,000).

Located on the northern shores of Lake Victoria at an altitude of 4,300 feet (1,310 m) above sea level, Kampala is the heart of Uganda. It is the capital city, the largest urban center, the center of commercial life, and the seat of government. Kampala is spread over several hills. Its origins go back to 1891 when the kabaka ("ka-BA-ka," king) of Buganda had his court on Mengo Hill, which was then called "the hill of antelopes." The town grew to municipal status in 1950 and became a city in 1962. The climate of Kampala is typical of an inland tropical city. Temperatures range from a high of 81°F (27°C) to a low of 63°F (17°C), depending on the season.

Kampala has retained a traditional charm and is the greenest city in Africa. It is a vibrant modern metropolis adorned with gardens and parks. The Parliament Building and the National Assembly are located in

16

Kampala, as is Makerere University, the oldest and most prestigious university in East Africa. The National Theater is the most important place for cultural entertainment in Kampala, and people come from all corners of the city to enjoy performances of various kinds. The Botanical Gardens, started in 1898, were originally natural forest that was used as a research center for the introduction of various exotic fruits and plants to Uganda. Many of these fruits can be bought fresh in Kampala's Nakasero market.

Jinja is a major commercial center and the second largest city in Uganda. It is situated on the banks of Lake Victoria at the source of the Nile, 50 miles (80 km) east of Kampala. Jinja is the home of the Owen Falls Dam, a magnificent example of modern engineering that supplies power to most of Uganda and parts of Kenya and Rwanda. Jinja is a good center for exploring the central part of the country, including the raging Bujagali waterfall, which is located 6 miles (10 km) north of the city, and the source of the Nile 1.8 miles (3 km) away, with its monument to John Speke, the first European ever to set eyes on the site in 1862.

Evidence of Uganda's colonial heritage can be seen in the buildings on Jinja's main street.

HISTORY

AS UGANDAN HISTORY HAS ONLY BEEN DOCUMENTED from recent times, written evidence of Uganda's past goes back only 150 years. Nevertheless, oral traditions were important long before this, and from these much can be learned about what happened in Uganda several hundred years ago. Uganda has a long history, and the country seems to have been inhabited very early. Bantu people were engaged in agriculture there from as early as 1000 B.C. and iron working can be traced back to A.D. 1000.

During the 17th and 18th centuries powerful social and political orders developed, including the Bunyoro, Buganda, Busoga, Ankole, and Toro kingdoms, which made profitable links with the Sudanese slave trade that underpinned the regional economy. By the 19th century the kingdom of Buganda, the biggest area in Uganda, was allied to the powerful Shiraziz of Zanzibar and gained control over the other smaller kingdoms in the region. A hereditary kabaka (traditional prince) ruled the Baganda people, advised by a council drawn from the higher caste members of the tribe.

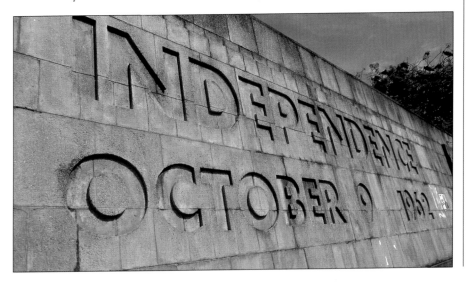

Opposite: **Children visit the Royal Tombs of the Kabaka, the traditional burial place of the leaders of the Baganda people.**

Left: **This wall was built to celebrate Ugandan independence in 1962.**

19

Mutesa I, the king of Buganda, reviews his troops. British explorer Captain John Speke looks on.

KING MUTESA I OF BUGANDA

Although there were many tribes and people of different ethnic origins in the area that is now Uganda, for many years the Kingdom of Buganda represented the real power in the land, and the king, or kabaka, was the supreme authority with power over the life and death of his subjects. From its rise to power sometime in the 1600s, Buganda and its kings followed traditional ways of doing things, with very little interference from outside influences, but by the third quarter of the 19th century, this was no longer the case in the Bugandan kingdom.

King Mutesa I was the last of the great kings of the Bantu tribe during the period of its dominance, and as so many changes took place so quickly during his reign, he was intuitively aware that he would probably be the last independent ruler of Buganda. The major decisions that had to be made during his reign were brought about by the increasing numbers of

Europeans, particularly missionaries, who were coming to his kingdom. Mutesa I's greatness lies in the fact that he gave shape to the aspirations of his people by controlling and even being the architect of many of these changes. He enriched his country by encouraging trade with the Arabs and others, and by peacefully opening up his country to new civilizations and cultures. There is little doubt that modern Uganda enjoyed its pre-independence colonial status as a British protectorate very largely because of what Mutesa I had done.

Mutesa I's wisdom as a king was recognized far and wide and many disputes were referred to him by his neighbors for arbitration. Many explorers, missionaries, historians, and colonial administrators who knew him well documented Mutesa I's personality as generous and hospitable.

When Mutesa I died, a fundamental change came over his kingdom. His death was the beginning of the end of Buganda. It was the start of the colonial era and the end of Buganda's existence as an independent state. The people of Buganda knew that things would never be the same again. Mutesa I was a good king—he died as a hero to his people and an international figure.

Mutesa I's successor, Mwanga, became kabaka of Buganda in 1884. He was a weaker character than his predecessor, and became jealous of the power and influence the missionaries had gained during Mutesa I's reign. In 1888 his efforts to banish them failed and he was deposed.

BUGANDA'S NEIGHBORS

Neighboring small states were happy to have Mutesa as king of Buganda, too, for he often acted as their protector. Bwera, Kooki, Toro, and a number of regions south of Lake Victoria, for example, were Buganda's "protected states." Whenever Kabarega (the king of Bunyoro) struck at Toro, a rebellious part of his kingdom, the rulers of Toro and many members of the royal family received military aid from Buganda and even took refuge there. If there is a state in modern Uganda that owes its existence to Buganda, it is the kingdom of Toro.

Captain John Speke introduces a fellow explorer to a tribal queen in 1864.

EUROPEANS IN UGANDA

In the 1830s Arab traders came to Uganda from their traditional bases on the Indian coast of Africa, shortly followed by British explorers looking for the source of the Nile, the first of whom was Captain John Speke in 1862. English Protestant and French Catholic missionaries arrived soon after at the request of Kabaka Mutesa I, and Baganda loyalties split into "French" (Catholic), "English" (Protestant), and Muslim parties.

In 1888 the Imperial British East Africa Company was set up in Buganda with the kabaka's permission, and in 1894 Buganda was declared a British protectorate. In 1896 the kingdoms of Bunyoro, Ankole, and Toro also became British protectorates, and Buganda's administrative system was extended by the British to these societies. In 1905 Uganda was put under the direct control of the British Foreign Office.

Uganda was never fully colonized, as non-Africans were not allowed to acquire freeholds, that is, to own land. By 1913, with the completion of the Busoga railroad, the cotton industry was well established, and by

The 1920s, coffee and sugar were also grown commercially. A legislative and an executive council were set up in 1921. In 1961 a special constitutional conference on Uganda was held in London and a timetable for independence was formally established.

The colonial style of architecture of many of the old buildings in Kampala dates the short period in which Uganda was under British rule.

JOHN SPEKE

John Speke, one of the early explorers of the African continent, was born in England in 1827. After serving in the British Army in India, he went to Africa in 1854 with another explorer Richard Burton, where they became the first Europeans to sight Lake Tanganyika in 1858. After this discovery, Speke traveled farther into the interior of Africa by himself, eventually coming across a large lake, which he named Victoria, and further claiming it to be the source of the Nile river. His assertions about Lake Victoria were not believed in England at first, and so he mounted a second expedition to the same area between 1860 and 1863. He never got a chance to defend his claims a second time, as shortly after his return to England in 1864, he was killed in a shooting accident.

The Uganda parliament building on the day when the Kabaka of Uganda presented gifts to the Duke and Duchess of Kent of England after the country's independence was formalized.

UGANDAN INDEPENDENCE

During World War II, for the first time, Uganda was faced with the task of becoming as self-sufficient as possible because the British were focused on defeating the Germans. After the end of the war in 1945, the first Africans were nominated to the Legislative Council, and in succeeding years, there was a steady increase in African representation. In 1954 African membership was increased to 14 out of a total of 28 nonofficial members. The 14 were selected to represent districts thought to be more natural units of representation than the British-created provinces that had previously been established. In 1955 a ministerial system was introduced, with five official African ministers out of 11. The success of the council was undermined, however, by Buganda's erratic participation—a legislature was seen as a threat to the degree of autonomy that Buganda wanted for itself. This feeling was strengthened when Mutesa II was deported in 1953 for refusing to cooperate with the colonial government. He returned in

1955 as a constitutional ruler, but relations between Buganda and the protectorate government remained lukewarm at best.

In the late 1950s, with the emergence of a few African political parties, the African population concentrated on achieving self government. However, because of the poor organization of the parties and the fact they were based in Buganda, efforts were focused on the legislative council, where the other parts of the country felt themselves better represented. The Kingdom of Buganda intermittently pressed for independence from Uganda, and the question of the country's future became crucial. Finally, discussions in London in 1961 led to full internal self-government in March 1962. Benedicto Kiwanuka became the first prime minister. Uganda finally became fully independent on October 9, 1962. In the general election held later that year, the Uganda People's Congress (UPC) gained the majority under its leader Milton Obote. Obote began to act in a more and more dictatorial way, eventually abolishing the traditional kingdoms and proclaiming Uganda a republic. Obote remained in power until 1971 when a military coup was staged by former paratroop sergeant Idi Amin Dada.

During Idi Amin Dada's presidency, there were many wars, both within Uganda and between neighboring nations.

Idi Amin Dada in full military dress during his reign as Ugandan president during the 1970s.

IDI AMIN DADA

Amin was a member of the Kakwa tribe of northwestern Uganda. He did not get a formal education and joined the King's African Rifles of the British colonial army in 1943. He served in the army during World War II, and fought against the Mau Mau revolt in Kenya from 1952 to 1956.

He was one of the few Ugandan soldiers to be promoted to the status of officer before Ugandan independence in 1962 and became a close ally of the country's new leader, Obote. The good relations he enjoyed with Obote, however, did not last, and in 1971 Amin took over power following a well planned military coup. He became president and leader of the armed forces and in 1976 declared himself president for life.

Amin's rule depended heavily on violence, and one of his most brutal acts was slaughtering a group of Obote's loyal army officers. One of his biggest mistakes was ordering the expulsion of Uganda's Asian community in 1972. He had not anticipated how destructive this move would be economically, as the Asian community provided Uganda with essential commercial expertise.

Murder, destruction of property, looting, and rape increasingly became the hallmarks of his troops. He also allegedly ordered the persecution of members of the Acholi and Lango tribes. When, in 1978, he annexed Tanzania's northern territories, he found himself at war. Tanzania's troops defeated Amin's army and his rule was over.

OBOTE VS. MUSEVENI

It was the Uganda National Liberation Army (UNLA), led by Oyite Ojok and Yoweri Museveni, which launched the invasion of Uganda that toppled Amin. The combined invasion forces were urged by Tanzania to unite and form an alternative successor to the government. This brought about the formation of the Uganda National Liberation Front (UNLF) in Tanzania, with Yusef Lule as leader. However, barely two months into power, Lule was voted out of office and replaced by Godfrey Binaisa, a former attorney general of Uganda. Binaisa was dismissed a year later by the UNLF military commission and Obote was proclaimed president for a second time in December 1980.

The second rule of Obote was disastrous for Uganda. There was widespread violence and rampant murders. During the election campaign, Museveni had repeatedly vowed that if the elections were not conducted fairly, he would wage war on Obote. True to his word, and starting with only 27 men, Museveni formed the National Resistance Army (NRA) and began a guerilla war. Finally, officers from the Acholi tribe deposed Obote from power for a second time.

The NRA took control on January 26, 1986, and Museveni (who was still the president in 1999) was sworn in as president three days later. President Museveni began a visible effort to build national consensus and promote reconciliation, while at the same time dealing firmly with the remnants of the defeated armies. A National Resistance Council (NRC) was established with civilian and military representatives. This council developed and applied a system of resistance committees throughout the entire structure of government, so that, for the first time in history, people were able to elect their true representatives and there was a visible effort to maintain discipline among the military forces.

Oyite Ojok, Milton Obote's cousin, was killed in a helicopter crash during Obote's second rule, gravely weakening Obote's position.

BURIAL PLACES

In the area surrounding Kampala, which was for many years the tribal capital of Buganda, many of the former kings have burial places that can be visited. The most well-known of these are the Kasubi tombs, 3 miles (5 km) northwest of Kampala on the Hoima road where four revered kabakas, Mutesa I, Mwanga, Duadi Chwa, and Mutesa II are buried. This historic site was once the center of the Buganda Kingdom.

The Kasubi tombs rank among the finest monuments in Kampala—this historic resting place of the kabakas of Buganda is a fine example of the traditional skills and craftsmanship of the Baganda in building and architecture.

OTHER HISTORIC SITES

Kabalega's tomb is another historic site. Kabalega was the ruler of the Bunyoro from 1869 until he was exiled by the British in 1899. He returned to Uganda in 1923 and died at Jinja. The Karambi tombs in Kabarole are the tombs of Daudi Kyebambe (Kasagama) and George Kamurasi Rukidi II. The Kingdom of Toro arose in the early 19th century when Prince Kaboyo, son of the ruler of Bunyoro Daudi Kyebambe, rebelled against his father. Kalema's Prison ditch, 10 miles (16 km) west of Kampala, is another burial ground. Kabaka Kalema (1888–90), a Muslim who reigned during times of religious strife having succeeded his brother to the throne, had 30 close relatives killed in this ditch.

The Kasaba tombs are made of reeds and bamboo poles, and are lined with bark cloth.

GOVERNMENT

THE PEOPLE OF UGANDA HAVE HAD MANY TYPES OF GOVERNMENT during their long history, but until the coming of British colonialism, there was no central government. Originally government was in the hands of the tribal groups, who elected their own elders and made their own laws, which all members of their group were expected to follow. Later some central authority was given to the kings of the various tribes, including the largest of these, the Baganda, whose ruler, the kabaka, was considered the king and had ultimate authority over his people and their land.

Nowadays, the Republic of Uganda is headed by President Yoweri Kaguta Museveni, who leads the National Resistance Movement (NRM) which has governed the country since the overthrow of former president Obote in 1986. The legislative body (parliament) is called the National Resistance Council and is made up of 268 members elected by all Ugandans.

Opposite: **A statue of Bugandan King Ronal outside Parliament Building in Kampala.**

Left: **The entrance to the National Assembly building in Kampala.**

The kabaka of Buganda, Mutesa II, inspects the police guard after inaugurating the High Court of Buganda.

MUTESA II

Mutesa II, whose full name was Sir Edward Frederick William David Walugembe Mutebi Luwangula Mutesa, was the kabaka of the East African State of Buganda (now part of Uganda) from 1939 to 1953, and again from 1955 to 1966.

During the 1940s, although he was nominally king, Mutesa was essentially controlled by the British resident and his katikiro (prime minister) and was personally unpopular. In 1953, when elimination of the privileged position of King of Buganda within the protectorate of Uganda seemed imminent, Mutesa II took an unyielding stand in meetings with the governor of Uganda so as not to completely alienate many of his increasingly suspicious and anti-British subjects. His key demands were for separation of Buganda from the rest of Uganda and the promise of independence. When he refused to communicate the British government's formal recommendation (which would have deposed him) to his lukiiko (parliament), he was arrested and deported.

A KING IN EXILE

Buganda leaders engineered Mutesa II's return in 1955, as a constitutional monarch who still had a great deal of influence in the Buganda government. When Uganda became independent, Prime Minister Obote hoped to placate the Baganda by encouraging Mutesa's election as president in 1963, but a conflict over the continued integrity of the Buganda kingdom with Uganda followed. When Mutesa II tried to incite trouble between the traditionally stateless northerners and the southern "kingdom" members, Obote suspended the constitution. The conflict between the two men escalated rapidly. Eventually Mutesa II was forced to flee to Britain in 1966 where he died in exile.

Ugandans flock to vote at local elections.

Yoweri Museveni, Uganda's president, is a man with strong opinions and a keen sense of right and wrong.

NATIONAL AND LOCAL STRUCTURES

There are 39 districts in Uganda for administrative purposes, each headed by a resident district commissioner (RDC) and chief administrative officer (CAO). Government services are provided by technical district officers who represent their ministries at that level. The urban authorities are comprised of Kampala City Council (KCC), 13 municipal councils, and 18 town boards.

At the local level, there is a council system that divides each district into five zones: village, parish, county, sub-county, and district. The village council is made up of all residents of a given area, with an executive committee of nine officials. All village executive committee members within a parish, constitute a parish council.

THE MAN AT THE CENTER

Current Ugandan president, Yoweri Kaguta Museveni, was born in 1944 during World War II. His name comes from the word *Abaseveni*, the local name for Ugandan servicemen in the Seventh Division of the King's African Rifles, in which many East Africans had been drafted. He was born in the countryside in Ankole, western Uganda, and because the peasants in his home area were nomads, he did not go to school when he was young. Modern ideas about hygiene and health care had not been introduced to the people of his area, who were exploited and oppressed by land policies, including ranching policies instituted by the British and supported at first by some local chiefs and later by some neocolonial politicians. As a result of his background, Museveni became determined at an early age to fight against political and social injustices.

In the government that succeeded Idi Amin, Museveni served briefly as Minister of Defense. After Obote rigged the general election in 1980, Museveni opposed the tyranny of the Obote regime. During the struggle, Museveni's troops achieved a very high level of leadership and managerial skills, as well as clear political and military policies. They also established excellent working relations with the civilian population in areas where they operated. After a five-year guerilla war against the regimes of Obote and his successor Tito Okello, Museveni became president of Uganda on January 26, 1986. He formed a broad-based government in which formerly hostile factions were brought under the unifying influence of the National Resistance Movement (NRM). His reading of liberal Western thinkers such as American economist John Kenneth Galbraith shaped his intellectual and political outlook.

Milton Obote on his return to power in 1980.

ECONOMY

UGANDA NOW HAS A FREE-MARKET ECONOMY. The government is in the process of privatizing many of the formerly government-run enterprises to improve the quality of goods and services they provide. It also recognizes the need to attract both local and foreign investors who can supply capital, modern technology, managerial skills, and international marketing expertise to achieve its objectives.

AGRICULTURE

Agriculture still dominates the economy of Uganda, accounting for 44% of the GDP in 1996, 90% of export earnings, and about 80% of employment. Uganda has an ideal climate and extremely rich soil for growing crops, although only one third of the estimated area of cultivatable land is utilized.

Opposite: **Coffee is an important crop in Uganda.**

Left: **Harvest time on one of the many vast tea plantations in the Ugandan countryside.**

Visitors come from all over the world to try and spot as many varieties of wildlife as they can in Uganda's national parks.

TOURISM

Tourism is one of the fastest growing sectors of the economy at the present time, and an industry with great potential. The Ministry of Tourism, Wildlife, and Antiquities has recently drawn up a package of policy measures geared toward the development of all aspects of tourism resources in Uganda.

Visitors to Uganda can enjoy many outstanding attractions, such as the numerous national parks and game reserves that provide unsurpassed viewing of the varied animal, bird, and plant species. Other attractions include the source of the Nile at Jinja where it begins its 1,860 mile (3,000 km) journey to the Mediterranean, the extremely rare and endangered mountain gorillas in the Muhavura range, the spectacular Murchison Falls on the Nile, and the famous Ruwenzori Mountains that provide challenging climbing experiences. There is great competition for tourists by neighboring Kenya and Tanzania, which have established tourist industries. Uganda is striving to market itself as an equally appealing holiday destination.

These steel workers in Kampala supply goods to the building industry.

MANUFACTURING

The manufacturing sector has an important role in adding value to agricultural output, by producing food and beverages and developing local substitutes for imported goods, thus accelerating overall growth. At present, firms producing food, beverages, and tobacco employ about 45% of the labor force, followed by textiles, leather and footwear companies which employ about 16%. Other important industries produce furniture, cement, steel, processing for agricultural commodities, and soap.

There are also a number of specialized manufacturers of wholly Ugandan products that make a significant contribution to the country's economy. Among these are Mwera and Nakigalala Tea (over 2,000 metric tons of tea is produced by these two tea estates for the domestic and international markets), and Sukari Sugar, a joint venture with Nutrasweet Inc., a subsidiary of the Monsanto Group of the United States, which produces blends of sugar and asparatame, while The East African Glass Works produces hollow glassware, such as bottles, for the soft drink and

brewing industries. The Flour Mill produces edible flour primarily from corn and Kakira Confectionery manufactures a variety of candies for the domestic market with a planned diversification into toffees, chewing gum, and chocolates.

FISHING

Fishing is of growing importance in Uganda as lakes, rivers, and swamps cover 10.8 million acres (4.4 million ha) of the country, and fish contribute a high proportion of Uganda's protein needs. The private sector has taken a great interest in the fisheries and has developed facilities for fish farming, fish processing, and the export trade. Fisheries and forestry account for about 8% of Uganda's agricultural output.

MINING

In the 1960s minerals contributed 30% of Uganda's foreign exchange earnings. The main minerals exported were copper, gold, tin, wolfram, bismuth, tantalum, beryl, columbite, and phosphates. The country is believed to have economically viable deposits of gold. Mineral exports for the quarter ending June 1996 totalled US$15.2 million.

ENERGY

Energy is divided into four subsectors—petroleum, electricity, woodfuel, and new and renewable sources of energy. Due to increased demand and inadequate power cables, power interruptions and rationing are regularly experienced. To counter this shortfall, priority has been given to increasing Uganda's hydroelectric potential, which is estimated at 2,000 megawatts. The capacity of the biggest dam, Owen Falls, is 150 megawatts, but is being upgraded to 180 megawatts.

Owen Falls Dam is an outstanding example of modern engineering. The generating plant supplies power to most of Uganda and parts of Kenya and Rwanda.

Opposite: **Local men buy fresh fish on Lake Victoria.**

Below: **The hydroelectric dam at Owen Falls near Jinja.**

Uganda, Kenya, and Tanzania have reestablished the East African Cooperation with its headquarters in Tanzania. Significant progress has been made in creating an integrated market of over 80 million people. An East African passport has been launched to ease travel of the nationals of the three countries within the region.

FOREIGN TRADE

Uganda's exports are dominated by agricultural products, coffee being the most important. Nevertheless, exports of other nontraditional agricultural commodities such as beans, corn, and fish products, are on the rise. The leading nonagricultural exports have traditionally been gold and manufactured products.

Since independence, Uganda has sent most of its exports to Western Europe and the United States. Regional trade with East African countries has been small, but there are signs of an increase, especially in food exports. Most goods are shipped through Kenya, but an alternative route through Dar-es-Salaam in Tanzania is becoming more important.

COMESA

Uganda is a member of the Common Market for East and Southern Africa (COMESA), a regional economic organization. Benefits available to members are a reduction on normal customs duties on trade, an easing of restrictions on settlements between members, and the use of clearing houses.

A DEVELOPING ECONOMY

Uganda has a developing market economy, largely based on agriculture. Economic deterioration due to corruption, expulsion of foreign firms, and war costs was once a major problem, but this slowed considerably after the 1970s, although violence and civil unrest remained serious obstacles to economic recovery into the middle of the 1980s. The government's current economic recovery plan aims to provide greater encouragement and protection for foreign investors, strengthen the main export industries, and improve essential social services.

WORKING LIFE

Ugandan labor is plentiful, generally well-educated, and English-speaking. Although the country has one of the best educational systems in Africa, with reasonably well-developed commercial schools and colleges, wages are low by international standards.

In fact, because of past inflation, official wages have become inadequate to meet the rising cost of living. Wages and salaries paid in the private sector are generally higher than those paid by the public sector. Many wage and salary earners are only able to survive because they have access to cheap food supplies which are generally plentiful most of the year.

An employer must contribute an amount equal to 10% of an employee's gross salary to the National Social Security Fund (NSSF), and a further 5% is deducted from the employee's salary.

Expatriates can work in Uganda provided they obtain a work permit. Such permits are usually granted to foreign enterprises approved to operate in Uganda so long as the applicants are key personnel.

Uganda Airlines has an impressive fleet of planes that fly to cities all over the world.

TRANSPORTATION

The transportation and communications infrastructure in Uganda suffered heavily during the period of civil unrest. Roads and railways were destroyed during the troubled times, and it has taken the country a long time to recover. Recognizing the importance of the transportation network to the economic development of the country, the government has now implemented a transportation sector rehabilitation policy.

The Civil Aviation Authority was established in 1991 and operates as an independent body. Renovation of Entebbe International Airport has been completed. There are currently 14 international airlines serving the airport. Another airport is planned at Nakasongola to cater to investors in the proposed export processing zone. The national carrier, Uganda Airlines, which currently flies to Harare, Johannesburg, Nairobi, Kigali, Bujumbura, and Dar-es-Salaam, is earmarked for privatization. The government also plans to privatize the management of airports in order to enhance their efficiency.

The railroad system has 775 miles (1,249 km) of track and links with the Kenyan railroad to Mombasa. There are train services across Lake Victoria from Jinja in Uganda to Mwanza in Tanzania and to Kisumu in Kenya. The Uganda Railways Corporation (URC) provides both passenger and freight services, but they are not always reliable as there are still serious operational difficulties resulting from the sustained heavy losses over recent years. The government is now taking steps to reorganize the activities of the URC, including closure of money-losing routes.

Most of the 1,240 miles (2,000 km) of the bitumen-surfaced highway network in Uganda has been repaired, and there is long-distance and local bus service to most towns and cities in Uganda, and to many of the smaller rural areas as well. In addition, 2,670 miles (4,300 km) out of 3,720 miles (6,000 km) of gravel highways and 12,420 miles (20,000 km) of feeder roads have been upgraded.

Most of the major lakes in Uganda have ferry services that crisscross the lake and link the small islands to the mainland.

Kampala's railway station is the central point for Uganda's railway network.

UGANDANS

THE 1991 NATIONAL CENSUS put the population of Uganda at 16.6 million, while the World Population Report of May 1997 estimated it to be 20.8 million. Population growth is currently 2.6% per annum, and the population is expected to grow to 22.2 million by the year 2000. Uganda's population is largely rural with about 90% of the people residing in the countryside. The population of Kampala was estimated to be 800,000 at the end of 1996. Average life expectancy is 44.9 years—43.6 years for men and 46.2 years for women. The fertility rate for women is 7.5 children. Uganda has one of the world's highest fertility rates which is reflected in its rapidly growing population.

The Asian deportations in 1972 resulted in an exodus by most of the resident Europeans and North Americans so today the expatriate population is still relatively small.

Opposite: **Women and boys from the Bakiga tribe in the Rukungiri district of western Uganda.**

Left: **Ugandan women with heavy headloads near Kabale in southwest Uganda.**

A CULTURE OF CONTRASTS

Uganda is a country of many contrasts. Just as the rugged mountains act as a foil to the broad savannas, and the dry uplands contrast with the wetlands of the lakeshores, so do the contrasts between the various peoples of Uganda reflect the variety of their surroundings. This is well demonstrated in the multiplicity of cultures, traditions, and lifestyles, which means that there is really no single Ugandan culture. Uganda is a melting pot of many different cultures.

The nation of Uganda is a result of the unification of several ancient kingdoms, as well as many smaller independent societies. Nevertheless, from their ethnic origins, Uganda's people can be divided in four different groups in terms of both their language and where the majority of them live. These four groups are the Bantu, the Luo, the Nilo Hamites, and the Sudanic.

A division is made between the Bantu South, where the Baganda, Basoga, Bagwe, Bagisu, Banyole, Basamia, and Kenyi ethnic groups live, and the Nilotic North, home to the Western Nilotes, known as the Luo. The Acholi and Lango are the two largest subgroups from this group. The Baganda make up about 20% of the population, the Western Nilotes 15%, the Eastern Nilotes 12%, and the Sudanic 6%. As a result of colonial rule, power was concentrated in the south, and therefore the Bantu became the dominant force in modern Uganda.

BANTU PEOPLE

By far the biggest ethnic group are the Bantu, who can be found in east, central, west, and south Uganda, and constitute 50% of the population. They were the earliest group to migrate to Uganda from Central Africa. Originally the Bantu people were mainly hunters and gatherers. They are believed to have introduced agriculture to Uganda with crops such as millet and sorghum. Although they split into many different tribal groups and evolved different languages, the Bantu tribes share one important characteristic that makes them easily identifiable—the names of most of the Bantu tribal groups begin with the prefix "ba."

A group of Bantu siblings near their homestead.

A group of Ugandan women in traditional Baganda dress.

BAGANDA

Of all the Bantu groups, the biggest is the Baganda. This is traditionally a group with no fixed social divisions—any person of talent and ability can rise to a position of social importance. This does not mean that Baganda society has no classes—quite the opposite is true. At the bottom of the social stratum, was a class of people known as the *bakopi* ("BA-koh-pee," serfs) who owed their livelihood to the goodwill of the *baami* ("BAA-mee," chiefs) and the *balangira* ("BA-lan-gee-ra," princes).

Next were the *baami*. Interestingly, this status was not necessarily just hereditary, but could be obtained through distinguished services, ability, or by royal appointment. The *baami* were the middle class in Baganda society, while the highest class was the *balangira*, the aristocracy who based their right to rule on royal blood. At the very top in Bagandan society were the *kabaka* (the king), the *namasole* ("NA-ma-so-lay," the queen mother), and the *nalinya* ("na-LEEN-ya," the royal sister). Kings, chiefs, and the royal assembly often demanded superior respect.

THE PEOPLE OF THE NORTH

The Nilo Hamites and the Luo are found in north, east, and northeastern Uganda. The Nilo Hamites—who are sometimes also called the Lango—trace their origins to Ethiopia and are mainly pastoralists. Unlike the Bantu, the Nilo Hamite groups have developed characteristics that distinguish them from one another, such as speaking languages that are quite different from the original one that they shared as a group.

The Luo, which includes the Acholi, Alur, Jonam, and Japadhola tribes, migrated from southern Sudan. They live in west, north and east Uganda. The Acholi tribe were traditionally organized in chiefdoms, each under a hereditary ruler known as *rwot* ("RWOT"). The *rwot* was a link between the living and the dead and offered sacrifices to the ancestors on behalf of the people. The administrative structures of the Luo were similar to the precolonial kingdoms of Buganda, Bunyoro, Ankole, and Toro.

A modern Ugandan family wearing traditional Banyankole clothes.

The Sudanic speakers of West Nile originate from Sudan, but their culture and language indicate that they have become completely detached from their place of origin. Under colonialism, the Lugbara language was encouraged in elementary schools and as a result, this group tended to dominate the rest.

PYGMOIDS

Pygmoids are part of a group of people whose adult men grow to less than 5 feet (1.5 m) tall. The Pygmoids of Uganda are thought to be the closest relatives to stone age people living in Uganda. They live by hunting and gathering and they do not have permanent dwellings, tending to be semi-nomadic, camping for a time where food can be obtained.

The Batwa, for example, live mainly by begging from and working for the Bahutu and Batuusi as there is no longer much scope for survival by hunting and gathering, because of increased population and encroachment on gathering grounds. The Pygmoids are ethnically related to the pygmies of the Congo.

Pygmoids can be found in the districts of Bundibujo and Kasese, inhabiting the tropical forests of the Congo River Basin on the western Uganda-Zaire border, particularly in the parts adjoining the Ituri forest near the Ituri river, which has its source in the Bulega hills overlooking Lake Albert and River Semuliki. The Pygmoids are believed to have been the original inhabitants of the Ruwenzori mountain areas before the arrival of the Bantu. Their original home is said to have been the forests of the Congo and their language, which is unique to them, is called Kumbuti.

Pygmoid men and women dress in the same way. A belt is wound around the waist with a piece of bark cloth attached to it. The bark cloth is brought down between the legs and fixed against the belt in the front.

Opposite: **Pygmoid children.**

BARK CLOTH

Baganda traditional attire consists of a bark cloth wrapped from the chest to the feet and tied around the waist with a thick belt. Called a *kanzu* ("KAN-zoo"), the cloth is partly covered by another piece of bark cloth tied around the shoulders. Bark cloth is made from the inner layer of a tree's bark—a fibrous material that becomes more resistant and supple the more it is beaten.

Once the bark has been extracted from a tree, it is stripped of any remaining wood and rough bark. The bark is softened, either by soaking it in water or smoking it over a fire, and spread across a large, smooth branch and hammered with a thick piece of wood. As it is beaten, the bark expands. After the bark dries, it is dampened and hammered once more. It takes about two hours of hammering to soften a piece of bark enough for simple clothes to be fashioned out of it. Completed bark cloths are worn for a variety of ceremonies.

LIFESTYLE

ALTHOUGH UGANDANS ARE BECOMING MORE and more like each other through the influence of modern communications and increasing intermarriage between various tribal groups, most Ugandans still live in a wide variety of different ways that depend on where they live and what their tribal tradition has taught them is important.

Much of the lifestyle of Ugandans in the villages has changed dramatically as a result of modern-day ideas brought in through the media, such as newspapers and television. Nevertheless, many traditional practices and customs are still evident in the behavior and attitude of many Ugandans, particularly in the more isolated regions, where allegiance to a tribe and its beliefs can be more important than being a "modern" person. The family unit is the nucleus of Ugandan life in rural areas, and families live a very close-knit existence in small village communities.

Opposite: **Karamojong women making bricks.**

Left: **A Karamojong homestead near the town of Kaabong.**

Typical Ugandan homestead-style houses in a village near Jinja.

HOMESTEADS

Traditionally, among agricultural peoples (and also in some rural areas today), the residential pattern was one of scattered homesteads, each surrounded by its own arable land and some reserved pasture land. Round houses with wooden frames, mud walls, and grass-thatched, conical roofs were common throughout the region. Banana-fiber thatch was used in areas in which bananas were common. Economies were all essentially subsistence—each household raised its own food supply and made its own clothes and houses.

Specialization, other than iron-working, was not usual, although some individuals developed skills as part-time artisans in addition to their normal work as potters, wood-carvers, bark-cloth makers, and herbalists. Each village had a specially recognized man who was selected from among the elders and acted as an intermediary between them and the local tribal chiefs, in addition to settling village disputes. These traditions are still very much in evidence in the Uganda of today.

THE FAMILY STRUCTURE

Some kind of compound or family homestead was typical in almost every tribal village and is still the situation in many rural areas today. Each household is ruled by the family head, who lives with his wife or wives, his married sons and their wives and children, and sometimes younger brothers of the family head, all within a single, fenced enclosure. Variations of this occur when brothers, and sometimes paternal cousins, live together with their wives and children, or when an influential man attracts close clansmen and their wives. Even when a man has only one wife, he often also has his own separate house or room where he keeps his possessions and entertains visitors.

It is the moral as well as the economic responsibility for the family head to ensure the production of sufficient food for his household. The men clear the bush, while the women till the land. Men work together to build round, grass-thatched huts for shelter and practice barter trade among themselves and their neighbors.

The Ugandan family unit is large, and sometimes three, or even four, generations live together.

A mother and child from Kinoni, a township on the road between Kampala and Mbarara

WOMEN AND CHILDREN

Traditionally, the women of the house and their children were the nucleus of the family and the center of domestic activity. Each wife had her own house, sometimes partly or wholly fenced off, or at least her own room in the large house. She also had the primary responsibility of household management, child-rearing, food preparation, care of the sick and elderly, and family health and welfare.

A wife usually also had her own kitchen hearth, where she cooked for all the family, and she often also had her own food store or granary. Older children sometimes had separate sleeping houses in the larger domestic groups.

Today, Ugandan women living in urban areas have developed careers of their own and endeavor to juggle a home life with the demands of a job. As in any modern Western society, this can put a great strain on domestic life as few Ugandan men take on an equal share of household responsibilities.

BOYS AND GIRLS

In rural places, Ugandan boys are taught and trained to grow up into responsible men and, in some tribes, are often initiated into manhood by undergoing the ritual of circumcision. Boys acquire skills while working alongside their fathers, who train them in methods of herding, fighting, hunting, agriculture, and trade. If the father is a skilled craftsman, such as a blacksmith, his son learns the art by working with him. This helps explain why some skills, for instance iron-working, rainmaking, divination, healing, pottery, and other specialities, tend to be hereditary. As a result, the Okebu tribe are renowned iron workers, and the Banabbuddu of Buganda are bark-cloth makers. These skills are particular to individual clans.

Girls are groomed to grow up into responsible housewives. Their mothers instruct the young girls in the proper ways of cooking, basketry, pottery, childcare, dressing, and other functions related to managing the household.

59

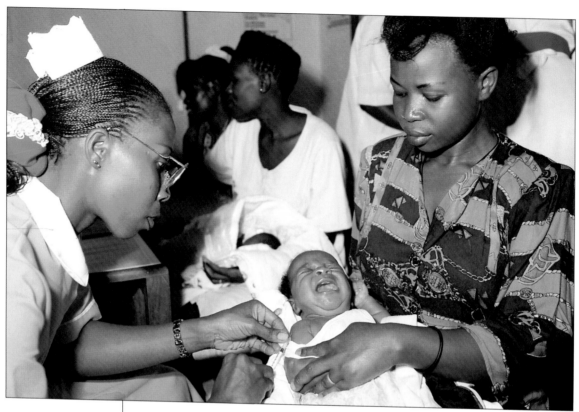

Above: **Young Ugandan mothers are aware of important health issues. This baby is being inoculated against infectious diseases.**

Opposite: **Some Ugandan women have children in their teens and become very young mothers.**

BIRTH

Traditionally, as soon as a Ugandan woman was married she was expected to conceive and give birth within a year. If this did not happen, questions would be asked, and if it took longer than what was considered "normal," the husband was at liberty to marry another woman.

Today, among the tribes, the more children one has, the wealthier one is considered. A woman is given more respect if she gives birth to a boy, because boys are the official heirs to their fathers. If a father has no boys among his children, he has to select an heir from his brother's sons.

Most women in rural areas give birth at home. After the birth the placenta is often buried, and the woman is confined to the home for a number of days. Sometimes she cannot even accept food from a member of her husband's clan until her days of confinement are over, although these practices are rare today.

Other customs associated with birth include confining a woman to the house until the umbilical cord has broken from the child's navel. The cords are sometimes kept in a special gourd, and the mother keeps the cords from all her children. In some tribes, women are also not allowed to look at the sky before the umbilical cord breaks off. A more extreme ritual involves killing a sheep by stomping on it until it dies to cleanse any taboos that are known to accompany the birth of twins.

The naming of a newborn child is done at a variety of times after the birth. Sometimes it can wait until the baby begins to cry continuously, but often the child is named immediately after birth by the father, mother, or grandfather of the child. Naming of the child also might wait until the umbilical cord falls off, when names are given by the grandmother or aunt of the child, or even until after the third day when it is named by the woman who helps in the delivery of the baby.

Some traditions even claim that an ancestor appears in a dream and dictates a name for the child—it might reflect the circumstances under which the child was born or be a day of the week, a place of birth, or the name of an ancestor.

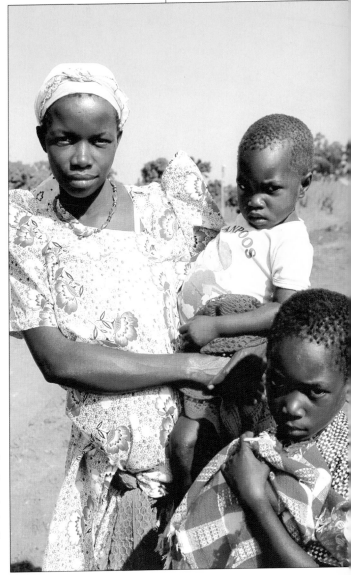

MARRIAGE

The biggest tribal group in Uganda, the Baganda, regard marriage as a very important part of life. Years ago, a woman was not respected until she was married, nor was a man regarded as being complete until he was married. As the Baganda are polygamous, allowing a man to marry more than once, the more wives a man had the more highly he was regarded in society.

In olden times, parents would initiate and also conduct marriage arrangements for their children. Before the marriage, an important clan ceremony, *okwanjula* ("ok-wan-JOO-la"), would be held. In this ceremony, the husband, escorted by his relatives and friends, would visit the relatives of the girl's side to introduce his line of clan and relatives.

In the event of a divorce, which was common in Buganda, the dowry would be repaid. The amount depended on the length of time the girl stayed married and whether she had any children within marriage. But today, young people are often allowed to make their choice of which partners to marry and arranged marriages are less common.

POLYGAMY

Among some of the other rural tribes today, marriage is also polygamous. The boy is usually consulted, and sometimes, the consent of the girl is required too, but often marriage is arranged by the parents of the boy and girl without the consent of either. Families often choose spouses early in life (normally when the boy is initiated), and some cultures demanded that all unmarried girls be virgins.

In the past, tribal groups had other forms of marriage that were also socially acceptable. With the Guturura or Gufata, the boy carried away the girl by force to be his wife. Another method was that boys of the same age would identify a particular girl and forcefully carry her to the home of the particular boy who desired her for marriage. When the boy slept with her, she became his wife, and further arrangements would then be made with the girl's parents. The reverse of this was *ukwijana* ("ook-wee-JA-na"), when a girl would sneak away from her parents and go to the boy's home to get married. Having a child before marriage was frowned on, but polygamy and divorce were usually readily acceptable. If a husband died, sometimes one of his brothers would take on his responsibilities, including his wives.

Opposite: **Dancers perform at a tribal "royal" wedding.**

THE ALUR MARRIAGE

One Ugandan tribe, the Alur, had a form of religious marriage. Tradition dictated that the man and the woman had to belong to the same religious cult to be socially accepted as a married couple. If they were not, the man had to be initiated into the woman's religion. If the couple subsequently divorced, the man would maintain the religious status he was given on his marriage.

DEATH

There are still a great number of superstitions attached to death among Ugandan tribes. Burial was usually after five days, after which there would follow a month of mourning. Ten days after the period of mourning there would be funeral rites known as *okwabya olumbe* ("ok-wa-by-YA o-LOOM-bay"), an important ceremony to which all clan elders and relatives were invited. Events included eating, drinking, dancing, and the installation of an heir. The heir would then take on the responsibilities of the deceased if he was the head of a family. In the same ceremony other cultural events would take place, such as *okwalula abaana* ("ok-wa-loo-LA ah-BA-na"), in which children would be formally identified as belonging to the clan and also given clan names (this is why in many cases Bagandas have more than two names).

The Banyankole believed death was attributed to sorcery, misfortune, and the spite of neighbors. The body remained in the house for as long as it took the relatives to gather before it was buried. During the days of mourning, neighbors and relatives remained at the home of the deceased. No digging or manual work was to be done as a consolation to the relatives of the deceased.

The Basoga had complicated death and burial rites. The process depended on the status of the dead. A chief was buried in the hut of his first wife with some of his belongings. A head of family's grave was dug in his own hut, garden, or courtyard, and an heir could be appointed at the time of burial. A childless man was despised in society and his name was not given to any children in the clan. A married woman was buried in a banana plantation. The relatives of the deceased were obligated to bring another unmarried girl for the widower. She became the heiress and took over the functions and property of the dead woman.

Other tribes followed similar customs, but with some variations. For instance, among the Banyole when a man died, there were three days of mourning during which there would be no bathing. If the dead person was a woman, the mourning would last four days. Among the Bagwe, if someone died everyone was expected to weep loudly or else they would be suspects in the cause of death.

The Banyoro feared death very much, as it was usually attributed to sorcerers, ghosts, and other malevolent nonhuman agents. Sometimes death was thought to be caused by the actions of bad neighbors, gossip, or slander. Burial would take place in the morning or afternoon.

The Baganda people did not believe that death was a natural consequence, and so all deaths were attributed to supernatural spirits.

Opposite: **Historically, Ugandan men have a shorter lifespan than their wives.**

UNUSUAL MOURNING RITUALS

Among the people of the Banyarwanda tribe, the death of a young person required special mourning rituals. There would be four days of mourning, during which no digging or manual labor by any members of the tribe was allowed.

When anyone died in the Japadola culture, the corpse would remain where it was overnight. Everyone else camped outside the house containing the dead body, and nobody was allowed to bathe for at least three days.

EDUCATION

The first education in Uganda was what the Europeans described as "informal education." This means that there were no defined institutions of learning, no trained teachers, no blackboards or pencils and books, but children could be taught all the same. In all the tribal societies, the system of education tended to be similar, only the subject matter or syllabus differed according to the particular need and social values of the given society. Through stories, tales, and riddles, the mother or grandmother would alert the children to what society expected of them as they grew up. Fathers would, through proverbs, stories, and direct instruction, teach their young sons their expected role in society.

But education was not only confined to discipline—it was considered an all-around process that catered to all facets of the individual. All that was taught was directed toward the creation of the ideal individual who would ably fit into the society in which he or she was born.

When the British arrived and colonized Uganda, the whole system of parents and elders educating and training the younger generations began to be discouraged. The arrival of missionaries and the establishment of missionary schools between 1840 and 1900 changed the education system. The first mission schools introduced formal education in which the emphasis was on writing, reading, and religion. All schools were operated by missions until 1922, when the British government assumed some responsibility for education by opening the first government technical school at Makerere (now Makerere University), emphasizing the liberal arts and sciences.

Makerere University is a highly regarded educational institution in Uganda.

Most Ugandan school-children have to wear a uniform.

THE EDUCATION MODEL

Unfortunately, the education system in Uganda suffered extensively during the long period of civil unrest and not everyone has been able to go to school. As a consequence, the literacy rate is very low—only about 50% in 1999. However, the government has recently passed the Universal Education Bill, which will ensure that every Ugandan child is in school by the year 2003 and will receive a good education. Today the Ugandan education system is based on a four-tier model, with seven years of elementary education followed by a four-year high school certificate. This leads to a two-year higher education certificate, a mandatory requirement for entry into a university, where a basic degree takes three years to complete. Some wealthy Ugandans choose to study for a degree abroad.

UGANDA TODAY

Modern Uganda is, on the surface, quite different from the old kingdoms that preceded it, although in many rural areas, life goes on in much the same way as it has done for hundreds of years.

It is in the Ugandan cities where the change from old to new is most obvious. In the traditional village many generations of one family lived together—or close by—as a tightly knit unit that provided assistance and support to anyone in the family who needed it. With many people moving to cities to find work in the last few decades, and the change in living conditions there, families have often been split up with the result that traditional support systems, especially for the young, no longer exist. This has led to more problems in families and a rising crime rate among young people. They no longer want to live the way their grandparents did but want to support themselves independently of their families—often in a society where work for the young increasingly demands the kind of education and training that few young Ugandans can afford.

This has led to an ever increasing gap between the rich and the poor in modern Uganda. This in turn fuels dissatisfaction among many people who feel that their future is blocked by the society in which they have been born.

But perhaps the biggest problem of all is that Ugandans still tend to think of themselves as members of their tribal group first and as Ugandans second. This is understandable given that Uganda is a creation of many different tribal groups and practices, but it does not help the growth of a country if its citizens tend to accentuate the differences between them rather than the things that they have in common.

With the annual growth rate at nearly 3%, Uganda's population is set to double in little more than two decades. Today, half the population is less than 15 years of age.

There is a sharp contrast between the shantytowns on the outskirts of Kampala, and the modern high-rise buildings of the city.

KNOWING THE RIGHT PEOPLE

Bribery and corruption are still evident in the way things are accomplished —it is sometimes easier to pass a little money under the table to get the license that you need than to work for it, and getting things done is sometimes not a matter of getting prepared as much as knowing how to influence the right people to make things easy for you.

Similarly, sometimes the easiest way to get a good job is to be related to someone with sufficient influence to get you what you want—which means that even those who have worked hard to qualify for a well-paying position, simply don't get it because someone's brother, nephew, or niece is given preference in hiring. It is also not uncommon to get a job by paying someone to give it to you!

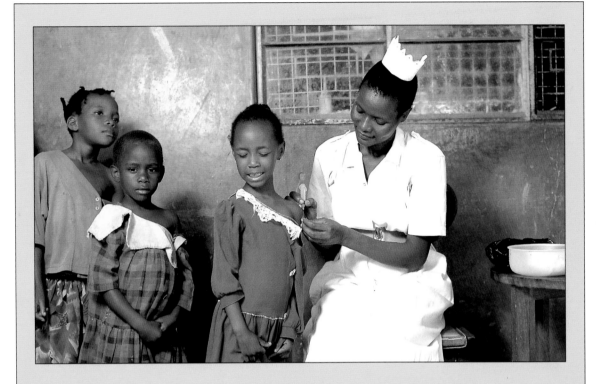

HEALTH

Health services in Uganda are available to all—though they are sometimes not as accessible in the rural areas as they are in the towns—and are provided by doctors, nurses, midwives, and health inspectors. In the last decade, the government allocated an average of 10% of its annual expenditure to health.

Following the departure of expatriate professionals under the Amin regime in 1972, the quality of healthcare provided by the government has declined. In 1960 there was one doctor for every 15,050 inhabitants, but by 1980 that number had increased to 22,291. As well as nearly 500 hospitals with just under 20,000 beds, the country's medical facilities include a school of hygiene, a department of preventive medicine, a disease-vector control unit, and a number of rural and city health centers.

Disease is still a major problem in Uganda. AIDS—which began on the African continent—has reached epidemic proportions and is a major killer among the Ugandan people despite campaigns for safe sex. Other easily transmissible diseases such as cholera and meningitis are still common—many of them caused through inadequate sanitation and poor hygiene. Diseases such as malaria, hookworm, venereal disease, and intestinal disorders are also common.

RELIGION

LIKE MOST THINGS IN UGANDA, religion was changed dramatically by the colonizing of the country in the 19th century. Traditional religions, though still practiced, are less common today. Religious tolerance, however, is an important part of present-day Uganda where Christians, Muslims, Jews, and Hindus are all free to practice their own religion.

TRADITIONAL RELIGION

The Baganda believed that Katonda was the creator, the supreme being who created the heavens and earth. Katonda was also believed to be one of the superhuman spirits who were divided into *mizimu* ("mi-ZEE-moo"), *misambwa* ("mi-SAM-bwa") and *balubaale* ("BA-loo-ba-lay").

The *mizimu* were believed to be the ghosts of dead people. When the body died, the soul would still exist as *mizimu*. Such ghosts would haunt anyone the dead person held a grudge against. If the *mizimu* entered natural objects, such as stones or trees, the *mizimu* would become *misambwa*, and at another level, *mizimus* could also become mythical tribal figures known as *balubaale*.

Like the Baganda, the Basoga believed in a supreme being, Lubaale, and several other gods and subgods. Human beings worked as messengers of their ancestors, Lubaale, or other gods. To the Basoga, the spirit world, places of worship, animated objects, and fetishes all had power to do good or evil to the living.

Opposite: **Lugaba Cathedral in Kampala with a statue of the Virgin Mary at its entrance.**

Above: **Nuns browse at a stall selling religious artifacts.**

73

Members of the Acholi tribe perform a religious dance.

JOK

The Acholi believed in a supreme being called Jok and in another god, Lubanga, who was the cause of evil. Lubanga had to be appeased at all times. The Acholi also worshipped the spirits of the dead and believed that they helped the surviving members of the family if they were treated well.

Like the Acholi, the Lugbara and Langi, the Jophadhola, and the Alur regarded Jok as a supreme being. They also believed in other gods known as Bandwa, the *jupa jogi* ("joo-PA jo-GEE") and *jupa jok* ("joo-PA jok"), as well as other spiritual entities and their dead ancestors. Worship was not routine, but necessitated by misfortunes or diseases. In case of a misfortune, the family head would approach a special diviner known as *julam bira* ("joo-LAM bee-RA"), *iolam wara* ("eye-oh-LAM wa-RA"), or *ajoga* ("eye-YO-ga"), to have the misfortune diagnosed.

ANCESTRAL SPIRITS

The Basamia and Bagwe people believed in a supreme being and in ancestral spirits who intervened in human affairs and caused harm, death, and misfortune if not appeased. Sacrifices were offered to them and each family had a shrine called *indaro* ("in-DA-ro").

The Bakonjo believed in two supreme beings, Kalisa and Nyabarika. Kalisa was half-man and half-monster. Nyabarika was believed to be the most powerful spirit being who had the power to heal, kill, haunt, provide fertility or cause barrenness, and make hunting expeditions successful or not. Since the Bakonjo regarded hunting as a very important activity, both for sport and as a source of food, skilled hunters enjoyed a position of importance in their society.

The Bagisu had a strong belief in witchcraft, coloring their outlook on the most ordinary events. They also believed that events were controlled by their ancestral spirits, and so it was important to keep them happy, too.

An unusual taboo existed within the Bakiga tribes–people. It was forbidden to sell any animals given as wedding presents—such animals could only be used to obtain wives for the girl's brothers or father.

TABOOS

Each tribe had its own rules, and the young were taught the do's and don'ts of the society in which they were born. Among the Basamia, Bagwe, Baganda, and Basoga, the taboos varied from clan to clan, but no one would eat flesh of the animal that was considered to be his lucky totem. Parents were not allowed to sleep in the same hut as their son-in-law, and once children were considered adults, they would not sleep in the same hut as their parents.

Among the Banyoro, pregnant women were not allowed to attend burials for fear that they might miscarry. Graves were marked with stones or iron rods so that nobody would build over them. If this happened, it was believed that all the members of the family would fall ill and then die.

The Kibuli Mosque in Kampala serves the population of Ugandan Muslims living in the city.

MODERN-DAY RELIGION

With the advent of colonialism and new foreign religions in the second half of the 19th century, the traditional cultural setup of different Ugandan societies was transformed. With the introduction of Islam and Christianity, it became fashionable to communicate with God in Arabic, Latin, and English. The manner of worship changed greatly as traditional shrines were replaced with mosques or churches with seats, church organs, and electricity. Prayers became regular on Fridays for Muslims and on Sundays for Christians, and no longer depended on particular instances of want or trouble. Gradually, organized religion became a belief and a way of life.

Traditional African values began to be severely undermined by colonialism to the extent that those who became greatly engrossed in religion and education came to despise the traditional ways of life. There is still a great divide between the followers of traditional African religions and religions brought to Uganda from outside in terms of their beliefs, but each one accepts the other and respects their ideals.

MISSIONARIES

The arrival of the first Christian missionaries, Anglican and Catholic, took place in the kingdom of Buganda. Their message later spread to the rest of the country. The introduction of Christianity set the stage for new developments and marked a turning point in the religious life of the people, particularly the Baganda, as well as in the political structure of the Buganda kingdom and the region at large. Christian beliefs and attitudes prompted a social revolution that was to transform all aspects of local people's lives. The events that followed, unpredictable as they were, added to the discomfort the new changes had brought about.

An old church in western Uganda built when the first missionaries arrived in the country.

A busy Sunday morning at Nambirembe Cathedral in Uganda.

CHRISTIANITY

The Christian religion was received with much excitement by Ugandans, but converting imposed requirements. As doctrine denounced all native religious behavior and practices as heathen and satanic, becoming a Christian meant breaking away completely from one's old lifestyle, and adjusting to new moral and religious standards. New believers, called *abasomi* ("ah-ba-SO-mee"), or readers, were regarded as social rebels who had transferred their loyalty to a new religious system, thus turning their backs on the old tribal traditions.

With the backing of missionaries and their connections to the British government and its military might, Protestant and Roman Catholic converts were able to divide the Buganda kingdom, ruling it through a figurehead king dependent on their guns and goodwill. Thus, the foreign religions disrupted, divided, and transformed the traditional state, and made it easy prey for the ravages of imperialism that followed.

Nevertheless, the traditionalists fought back, and campaigns against Christian converts escalated, resulting in the execution of 26 Christians on June 3, 1886. Rather than deter the growth of Christianity, the martyrdom of these early believers seemed to spark its growth. As has been observed in many other instances, the blood of Christian martyrs only helped to promote Christianity's foothold, and Christianity (in all its various styles), is now the dominant faith in Uganda.

A Catholic nun discusses religious values with Ugandan students.

ISLAM

Although the majority of Ugandans today are Christians, there are still a number of people who follow the Muslim faith. Some Muslims are descendants of the early traders who came to Uganda before the arrival of Christianity while others are immigrants from nearby countries where Islam is the main religion. Most major Ugandan cities have at least one mosque.

JUDAISM

There is a community of black Ugandans living in eastern Uganda who practice Judaism. This group is commonly known as Abayudaya. They observe Jewish holidays and dietary laws, sing Hebrew songs, and keep the Sabbath holy, as Jews have for generations. This all started in the early part of the 20th century, when a well-known Buganda leader named

Semei Kakungulu resisted both the European colonialists and the missionaries with whom he came into contact. Kakungulu read of the Jewish faith, met several European Jews working in the British protectorate, and was eager to read, learn, and practice. During the 1920s, a European Jewish trader met Kakungulu and taught the community the theory and practice of the Jewish faith. In 1992 two Americans visited the Abayudaya for the Sabbath and were urged to send more visitors. Since then, many more have visited the isolated community, including two rabbis and a delegation of American Jews.

HINDUISM

Most of the practicing Hindus came to Uganda originally from the Indian subcontinent to open stores and run businesses, which they did very successfully. During the years when Idi Amin was in power, many of these business people were expelled from Uganda. However, their places of worship were not touched, and now that many of them have returned to Uganda, the Hindu temples are once again active places of worship and are as accepted a part of the religious landscape of Uganda as are the many Christian churches.

LANGUAGE

AS A COUNTRY WITH A MULTICULTURAL SOCIETY, a total of 46 different languages are spoken in Uganda. But there are just two official languages—English and Kiswahili.

English was only introduced to the country in the last century. Today, half the radio programs and newspapers are in English, which is also taught in all Ugandan elementary schools and spoken in the law courts. English, however, is not widely used outside of the major towns and cities.

Kiswahili, the other official language, originated on the coast of Africa about 1,000 years ago and was also imported into Uganda quite recently, spreading along the African slave routes in the 19th century. The government plans to make Kiswahili a mandatory subject in schools as it is probably spoken by more Ugandans than any other language and often used by rural people to communicate with strangers from other parts of Uganda and surrounding countries.

Opposite: **The main language of the Bagisu tribe is Luganda, which is a widely-spoken second language in Uganda.**

Left: **Students at an international school in Kampala where children from different cultures study together.**

THE IMPORTANCE OF LUGANDA

Luganda is the most widely spoken second language in Uganda, after Kiswahili, as it is the language of the Baganda, the largest tribal group in the country. Luganda is spoken from the northwest shore of Lake Victoria and the Tanzanian border to Lake Kyoga, although mainly in Buganda province, in the central and southeast region.

Luganda developed over many centuries as a spoken language only. It has only existed in written form since the arrival of the Arabs and Europeans in the latter part of the 19th century. At first, Luganda did not have any standard spelling, and so it was difficult to read. In 1947 a conference was held in Uganda to standardize the language. Now it has a clearly determined form based on five vowel sounds and 21 different consonants. Luganda has both long and short consonant sounds, like the Japanese language.

Most shop signs in Uganda are written in English, a language that the majority of Ugandans can understand.

OTHER LANGUAGES

The other languages spoken in Uganda are used mainly in local areas and are sometimes used for instruction in elementary schools, for government campaigns, such as birth control or literacy, or on radio programs specially designed for people living in a specific area.

Among the tribal groups, languages include Soga (or Lusoga), which is spoken by the Basoga who live mainly between Lake Victoria and Lake Kyoga, and Gwere (or Lugwere), spoken by the Bagwe people. Gwere is commonly used in the home in addition to being a medium of instruction in the first two years of elementary school. Acholi is spoken by 4% of the population mainly in the north-central Acholi district, while Adhola is the most distinct of the Western Nilotic languages in Uganda.

Of the non-Ugandan languages, Hindi and Gujarati are commonly spoken among the Asian Hindu community who migrated to Uganda during the early part of the 20th century. It is also commonly used in newspapers and radio programs.

Children learn about cultures from all over the world at this school in Kampala.

THE SIGNIFICANCE OF NAMES

Names are very important in Uganda as they portray tribal and religious affiliations and sometimes signify what clan an individual belongs to. Due to religious influences, however, most people in Uganda have an Arab, Christian, or European name, which is more commonly used than their traditional name.

Traditional names vary from tribe to tribe. Just mentioning someone's name to a Ugandan is enough for him to know which tribe and what area of Uganda that person comes from.

The same names can often be handed down from generation to generation. Sometimes chosen names reflect the traditional beliefs of the area in which the child was born, and are the names of gods or spirits. Circumstances prevailing in the tribe at the time of someone's birth can give rise to other names such as Lutalo ("loo-TA-lo") meaning war, or Mirembe ("mee-REM-bay") meaning peace.

The Significance of Names

Names can also relate to the appearance of the child at birth (or wishes for what he or she will grow up to be) such as Makula ("ma-KOO-la"), which means beauty. Most common of all, is simply to call the child by the name of the day on which he was born, such as Balaza ("ba-LA-za") meaning Monday.

Multiple births give rise to special names, which vary from tribe to tribe. The Baganda, for instance, use Babirye and Nakato for girls, or Wasswa and Kato for boys. At the birth of the twins it was quite common for the father and mother to take on new names too—Nalongo indicates the mother of twins, while the father would be Salongo.

Traditions in naming children is still very much alive in Uganda today.

The television assembly line of Sembule Electronics is based in Kampala. The parts for the sets are imported from India.

THE ROLE OF THE MEDIA

Many people in Uganda own a radio, even in the villages, and listening to the radio is a popular pastime. Not nearly as many Ugandans own a television, however, as they are much more expensive and out of the reach of many people. Sometimes villages will have a communal television set located in a common area—or owned by one person—and villagers will gather there in the evening after dinner to watch television together and discuss local and national events.

Both television and radio broadcasts have played a major role in raising public awareness of daily events and unacceptable practice such as corruption. In the past, many civilians were oblivious to the atrocities and corruption that were going on around them.

The Home Service of Radio Uganda broadcasts programs and news for 18 hours every day in 22 local and international languages. There are also four private FM stations in Kampala that broadcast 24 hours a day, including the BBC World Service. Other radio stations include Radio Sanyu, Capital Radio, Radio Buganda (CBS), and Voice of Toro.

Television programs are on the air 24 hours a day with programs in English, Kiswahili, and Luganda. There are three local television stations—although the standard is far from sophisticated—and a pay TV channel, TV Sanyu, CTV, and Multi Choice Cable, for those with wider tastes. The state owned service is UTV (Uganda Television).

NEW VISION

The government-owned *New Vision* is the official daily newspaper. It competes with many privately-owned newspapers that now make the news all that more informative. The main daily newspapers are in English, such as *The Monitor Daily*, *New Vision Daily*, *Crusader*, *Star*, and *Express*, while there are also daily newspapers in Luganda such as *Bukedde*, *Ngabo*, *Munno*, *Taifa Empya*, and *Orumuli*. As the literacy rate in Uganda is still low, newspapers tend to be read more often by city people while the villages get their information from the radio, and sometimes the television.

International newspapers are available with a more representative report on news from around the world, but tend to be several days out of date and very expensive. The global trend toward using the Internet as a resource for obtaining the latest reports has not yet taken off in Uganda.

ARTS

UGANDANS ARE VERY SKILLED in creating works of art, through performance and through practical skills. Some Ugandans excel in dancing and singing or in creative expression, such as weaving, and making bark cloth and pottery. Others are excellent craftsmen who make highly decorative mats, a variety of baskets, pots and chairs, spears, shields, bows and arrows, as well as drums of various shapes and sizes and other musical instruments.

DANCE

Traditional dances in Uganda are a way of celebrating events, and they differ from one tribe to another. Like the prevalent cultures and languages, the similarities and/or differences in the kind of dances found in Uganda usually indicate their regions of origin. To the unaccustomed eye, some dances seem to vary only minutely from region to region, and yet a small difference in the performance can determine what occasion a dance signifies in participating cultures. Whether for marriage, birth, royalty, death, or circumcision, every type of dance was important and is still so today in many areas of Uganda.

The Baganda tribe have ceremonial dances such as *mbaga* ("m-BAG-ah"), *nankasa* ("nan-KA-sa"), and *olugunju* ("o-loo-GOON-joo"). The *mbaga* dance honors occasions such as weddings and royal gatherings, where the women and men often dance together in a choreographed manner. *Nankasa* is a popular dance performed in almost all occasions. The Banyoro are famous for their *lunyege* ("loon-YAY-gay") dance.

Opposite: **Baskets for sale at the side of the road near Entebbe.**

Above: **Bark cloth is popular for making craft artifacts. Here bark is being stripped from a mutuba tree.**

Drums play a vital role in traditional Ugandan dances.

ACHOLI DANCING

Acholi dancing is communal, and they have eight different and distinct types of dance—*bwola* ("bwo-LA"), *lalobaloba* ("la-lo-ba-LO-ba"), *otiti* ("o-TEE-tee"), *myel awal* ("my-EL a-WAHL"), *apiti* ("a-PEE-tee"), *labongo* ("la-BON-go"), *myel wanga* ("my-EL wan-GA"), and *atira* ("a-TEE-ra"). The *bwola* dance is the most important because it is the chief's dance and is only performed on his orders. The men form a large circle and each carries a drum. The movement of their feet matches rhythmically with the beating of the drums. The women dance separately inside the circle without beating drums. The dance has a leader who moves by himself within the circle and sets the time and leads the singing. He is regarded as an important person and traditionally was among the few in the community allowed to wear a leopard skin.

In the *lalobaloba* dance, people dance in a circle, but no drums are used. The men form an outer ring, while the women form an inner circle. All the dancers carry sticks.

In the *otiti* dance, all the men carry spears and shields, and the dancers encircle drums that are usually attached to a post in the middle of the arena. There is more shouting than singing! The *myel awal* dance is a funeral dance during which the women wail around the grave, while the men dance the *lalobaloba* carrying their spears and shields.

Labongo is a dance following a successful hunt performed while the hunters are still away from their homes. Men and women face each other in two lines and jump up and down while clapping their hands. In the *myel wanga* dance, the men sit down and play their harps while the women dance the *apiti* in front of them. The *atira* dance is now outdated, but was held on the eve of a battle.

The Bagisu are famous for their circumcision dance, *embalu* ("em-BAA-loo"). The men dance in a circle around their friends about to enter manhood, while the women dance around the circle with encouraging comments of bravery. Most relatives take part in this lively and enthusiastic dance.

MUSIC

Musical instruments play an important role in Ugandan communities. The most popular musical instrument is the drum, which is used almost everywhere in Uganda. Music would be incomplete without the drum—not only is it used as a musical instrument but also as a form of communication, in dances, ceremonies, and for traditional worship and healing rituals.

The traditional songs are usually dominated by lyrics about loved ones, legends, or daily incidents, and some well-known events from the past. Songs are tuneful and accompanied by instruments such as drums, xylophones, shakers, logs, windblown instruments, and string instruments.

Opposite: **Traders sell cheap audio equipment and other items at a market stall in Kampala.**

Below: **Many traditional Ugandan folk instruments are hand crafted using natural materials.**

FOREIGN INFLUENCES

Today, music adapted from that of other countries is also common in urban areas and on many radio stations. Most popular is *lingala* ("lin-GAA-la") music from neighboring Zaire, as well as West and South African music. Foreign artists performing soul, country, zouk, soca, reggae, rap, and calypso are also popular.

Most street markets have stalls selling audio equipment, blasting out music by bands from all over the world. Ugandans are not quiet people and enjoy the emotion invoked by a rhythmic beat.

FINE ARTS

The practice and appreciation of fine arts are limited to a small but expanding section of the population. The Makerere School of Fine Art has trained some of East Africa's leading painters, sculptors, and art teachers. The school also teaches industrial art and design.

African art styles are unique in their use of natural forms combined with a range of colors in tune with the lush vegetation and wildlife. It is a style less sophisticated than that of the Western art world, but is growing in popularity and stature in galleries around the world.

STORYTELLING

There is a strong tradition of oral storytelling within many tribal groups in Uganda. The stories vary from group to group, but the majority of the stories were told by grandparents to their grandchildren as part of their education within the family. These stories have survived intact for centuries, and Ugandan children today still love to listen to the elders of the family retelling these stories, in the same manner they were told a generation before.

Although some of these stories are very old, they were not written down until quite recently, as none of the tribes had a written language. And so it is hard to know for this reason how the stories started or what they actually refer to. However, most of the stories that survive are directed at children and have a moral that is meant to be learned from them. A great number of stories feature talking animals. Some of them are good characters who help children, but others are designed to be frightening and warn the children of the consequences of behaving badly or of not being brave. Curiously, a bear-like creature (there are no bears in Uganda) is the main scary monster in some of these tales!

Two of the best known stories are Nabweteme (The Forest), which shows the value of being courageous and brave under difficult circumstances, and Jogoli Jogoli (Disrespect), which illustrates the importance of listening to the instructions of one's parents!

TRADITIONAL CRAFTS

Traditional crafts are part of Ugandan culture and are the result of expressions and feelings of people responding to a variety of historical events and influences. Simple handicrafts such as baskets and mats can tell a story and can be identified with a particular tribe by the patterns they display. Crafts have developed through the diverse traditions of the people and vary widely by ethnic settings. Many crafts are also hereditary occupations in Uganda, and skills or techniques are learned in childhood while working alongside a parent or other adult. Certain clans are well known for specific crafts.

Ugandan crafts feature containers such as gourd and wood vessels, baskets, handmade mats and house decorations, and furniture.

Weaving is a popular trade and locally produced crafts are common souvenirs for tourists.

LEISURE

LEISURE ACTIVITIES IN UGANDA are a combination of traditional and simple pastimes that can be enjoyed by most of the population. Some of the activities are Ugandan in origin—others were introduced by foreigners during the colonial period.

The way people spend their leisure time depends on where they live, their position in society, and their economic circumstances. Residents in rural villages where homes may lack basic amenities such as electricity and running water, are more likely to spend their leisure time visiting neighbors where they will chat, gossip, or play simple traditional games. In villages where electricity is available, these leisure options would also include listening to the radio or even watching television. Sometimes, the gap between the poor and rich is so wide in Uganda that one family could have a satellite television in their house, while their immediate neighbor's home could lack even the basic amenities.

Opposite: **Young Ugandan children compete in a school race.**

Left: **Umweso** **("oom-WAY-soh") is a popular board game in Uganda.**

TRADITIONAL ENTERTAINMENT

Village social gatherings may include entertainers who begin their performances at dusk. Storytellers attract large crowds of listeners, while magicians, tumblers, acrobats, and skilled jugglers weave their way through the audience as it ebbs and flows.

There might be a snake charmer performing with a huge mesmerized snake or tamed monkeys that have been taught tricks to delight the crowd. People drift from one group to another, and there is continuous exciting activity, often done in the hope that the spectators will donate some money to the performer!

Ugandan children do not need expensive toys—this band is happy to make do with home-made instruments.

TRADITIONAL GAMES

Ugandan children today still enjoy the games their parents played when they were young, using little more than ropes, corncobs, or leaves. Wheel-rolling is played by opposing teams in the streets. The players stand opposite one another holding tanglers, made of two pieces of corncob on a long string. One of the players stands in the middle of the street and rolls a wheel down it, while other players try to stop the wheel with their tanglers. The player who stops it sings a song of triumph.

Some games are very simple. Dirt-building is played by small children in a pile of dirt. Each child has a small red seed with a dark spot on it from an olusiti tree. A long pile of dirt is made, and the players hide their seeds in it. The pile is divided into several separate piles and the opposing team guesses in which pile the seed is hidden. All the other piles, except two, are scattered. If a team guesses correctly, it takes charge of the game. If not, this is counted as a score against them.

FUN IN THE CITY

Storytelling is a popular pastime in Uganda. Children love to sit and listen while adults recount fables and stories they remember from their youth. Traditional tales have been adapted over the years, but the themes remain unchanged. The characters are often animals and the stories have a moral message.

Town and city dwellers, especially those who are wealthy, have more choices than those who live in rural areas. Over the last few decades, and during times of peace, facilities have been built to accommodate those demanding a higher standard of recreation. These activities might include a visit to the movies where international, as well as African, releases can be seen. There are also swimming pools or soccer stadiums where local matches are held each weekend.

In urban areas the gap between the rich and poor can be particularly wide. For the privileged few there is a choice of golf, tennis, or squash at members-only clubs. Municipal facilities are limited and outdated, so many prefer to entertain themselves at home. Children from poor families in the towns use the same initiative as those living in the countryside, and play traditional games together.

Going out as a family is not a Ugandan tradition—this idea has been imported from the Western world. It is still common, however, for women and children to go out on their own, and the men to go out separately. Couples are normally seen together in the evenings. Many men tend to congregate in cafés and bars to talk and sometimes exchange gossip over tea, coffee, or alcohol.

Although food is important in Ugandan tradition, eating out is not nearly as common as having friends or family in for a meal at home. Restaurants are mainly for workers at lunchtime, for business meetings, or for visitors to the area.

The older people of the community have little need for modern forms of entertainment and are happy to sit and talk, discussing subjects such as politics, religion, and the family. Men and women of this age group usually sit separately in a social environment.

Opposite: **Young Ugandan men enjoying international music at a Kampala discotheque.**

NIGHTLIFE

Urban evenings are filled with entertainment, with visits to discotheques and nightclubs, casinos, and movie theaters. This nightime entertainment, however, is only found in the large towns and cities of Uganda.

Bars and nightclubs are filled with local dancers and live bands that often play until long past midnight. Traditional entertainers can also be found in the Kisenyi and Nakivubo areas of Kampala.

SPORTS

Many Ugandans are avid sportsmen and sportswomen. Boxing was especially popular in the 1970s during the dictatorship of Idi Amin, who was himself a boxer. During this period Uganda produced several world champions, and the sport attracted the uneducated and underprivileged and later spread to the high schools. Boxing has declined in popularity in recent years, partly because of the general realization that injuries caused can be fatal.

Other popular sports include soccer, netball, swimming, tennis, golf, squash, rugby, and cricket.

Express FC play Kenya Breweries in the final of the Super Cup soccer competition.

SOCCER Soccer, commonly known as football, is the favorite sport of Ugandans. It is played in schools, villages, and towns and at all levels of society. In the villages it is typically played as a friendly match between villagers, while in the towns, matches tend to be between clubs or between different clans or tribal groups. There are few soccer stadiums in Uganda, but players are happy to practice on any field or clearing around towns or homesteads.

Soccer is also popular as a spectator sport, and many Ugandan soccer fans watch international matches between top European teams on television. Young boys can often be seen wearing the colors of their favorite team.

NETBALL Netball is tremendously popular among schoolgirls in Uganda. The game is played with seven players on each team, and the aim is to get the ball in the opposing team's hoop as many times as possible. The netball court is split by two lines that divide the court, and at each end of the court is a shooting semicircle and a 10 foot (3 m) goal post with no backboard. Scoring shots can only be taken from within this semicircle. Each team member has a designated position that is restricted to a specific area on the court. These restricted areas have both an attacking and defending player in them, one from each opposing team. Many Ugandan girls with a natural agility and athletic ability for sprinting make good netball players.

FESTIVALS

THERE ARE MANY REASONS TO CELEBRATE IN UGANDA. Some festivals commemorate traditional religious events, while others celebrate personal birthdays, wedding anniversaries, or graduation days. Also important are religious festivals such as Christmas and Easter for Christians, and Eid al-Fitr and Eid al-Adha for Muslims. Traditional festivals are celebrated alongside modern-day ones, creating a fascinating calendar of events during the year.

The crucial stages of life—birth, puberty, marriage, and death—have always been times of sacred significance to Ugandans, as they signify changes in the status of an individual and that person's relationship with fellow members of his society. In rural areas these celebrations take on a traditional form, and most are unique to each tribe or area. In large towns and cities, however, festivities for these occasions have adopted a Western style.

Opposite: **Dance is one of the many ways Ugandans celebrate festivals.**

Left: **Folk musicians perform in Independence Day celebrations.**

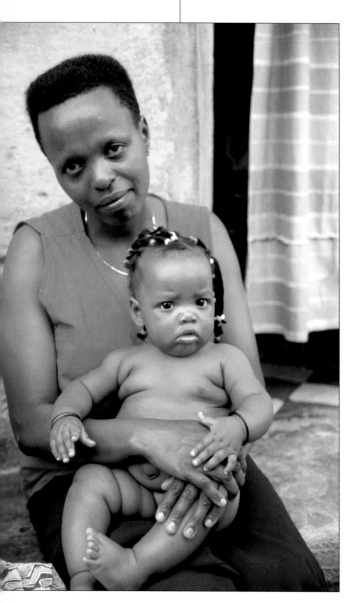

BIRTH

The naming ceremony of a newborn child can take place at a variety of times after the birth, but it is always an important reason to celebrate. Sometimes a celebration is held immediately after the child's birth, other times it is held when all the relatives can get together for a party with plenty of food, singing, and dancing.

In Christian families, the child is usually welcomed as a new member of the local church, as well as through the sacrament of baptism. This form of celebration, the contemporary christening ceremony, is performed regularly in Uganda for Christian families.

DEATH

Death requires numerous festival customs. Festivities surrounding funeral rites include the customs of playing mournful and sometimes joyful music, making speeches celebrating the life of the deceased, performing elaborate or simple embalming practices, and taking part in feasts of various kinds depending on the economic or social circumstances of the deceased or his next of kin.

FESTIVALS OF MARRIAGE

The rite of passage from the single to the married state is celebrated with many forms of festivals in Uganda. These ceremonies are often accompanied by feasting and gift-giving to express the pride of the community. The wedding festival welcomes the newlywed couple into successful participation in the community and its future expansion through the birth of children. Among most tribes, after the wedding, dancing and feasting lasts until well into the following day. The food is simple—meat stew with rice or corn—but plentiful, and is eaten outdoors.

Within certain tribes, it is customary to present large wedding gifts, such as the marital bed complete with new linen, pillows, and a bedspread, at the reception for the guests to admire.

Modern-day city weddings take the form of a religious service followed by a large reception for family and friends at home or at one of the many hotels in Kampala. This is a fairly formal occasion where a grand buffet is served to guests.

Above: **These children are part of the bride's entourage at a wealthy Kampalan wedding.**

Opposite: **Child naming is always a cause for a celebration in Uganda.**

RELIGIOUS HOLIDAYS

The major Christian and Muslim religious holidays are celebrated in Uganda in traditional ways. At Christmas and Easter, Christians go to church and exchange gifts. Eid al-Fitr, which marks the end of a month of fasting, is the most important Muslim holiday and is celebrated by Uganda's Muslims with feasts. Eid al-Adha marks the end of the holy pilgrimage.

A school band takes part in a Liberation Day parade.

SECULAR HOLIDAYS

Secular holidays in Uganda include:

LIBERATION DAY (January 26), which celebrates the coming to power of the National Resistance Movement. On that day, the head of state gives a speech to the people on the successes and failures of the country to date.

NATIONAL INDEPENDENCE DAY (October 9), the day Uganda became a self-governing republic.

INTERNATIONAL LABOR DAY (May 1)

INTERNATIONAL WOMEN'S DAY (March 8)

Ugandan schoolchildren rehearse a play celebrating Uganda's independence.

FOOD

BEFORE THE USE OF GAS AND ELECTRICITY IN UGANDA, kitchens were often built separately from the main house. Cooking was mainly done using firewood and charcoal, so a separate hut for cooking kept fumes and smoke away from the main building. This is still the case in villages today. However, in modern-day Ugandan houses, especially in the cities, kitchens are part of the main house and are complete with electrical appliances much like those in the West.

Although the food that is eaten by Ugandans today is similar to that eaten in Westernized countries in other parts of the world, in olden-day Uganda, the kind of food that people ate depended very much on the tribal culture in which they lived. While some cultures had very similar staple foods, others differed depending on what was available and, more importantly, what was considered socially acceptable to eat.

Opposite: **Peanuts and fruit in a market.**

Left: **Workers cook rice for students at an elementary school.**

Nile perch being smoked at an outdoor smoke oven in a fishing village on Lake Victoria.

TRIBAL FOOD

The staple foods cooked in a traditional Ugandan kitchen usually included meat (mainly from cattle and goats), fish, millet, sorghum, beans, berries of various kinds, potatoes, cassava, pumpkins, matoke (bananas), and milk products, such as cheese and curd. Some tribes also used defibrillated, or baked, blood for food, as it was believed that some of the characteristics of the animal that it came from would pass into those who ate it, often making them stronger or more powerful. This tradition is still practiced by some tribes.

COOKING IN THE OPEN AIR

In village homes, cooking was mainly done on open fires heated by animal dung, as this was the only fuel available. Traditional cooking and eating utensils included huge bamboo storage baskets, winnowing trays, grinding stones, mortars and pestles, mixing ladles, an assortment of pots and dishes, calabashes, and gourds of all shapes and sizes, both to eat from and as mixing bowls.

Modern utensils are becoming common, but many Ugandans still eat using their hands, taking the food from a communal pot and using small saucers for the food. Now that most Westernized packaged and processed foods are widely available, Ugandans have given up much of their traditional foods. However, they still enjoy eating local delicacies such as fried cassava, roasted sweet potatoes, steamed yams, and roasted corn. Cooking in the towns was often done in a similar way, but where available electricity and gas are now used as well as paraffin stoves.

FOOD RITUALS

Each tribe also had certain rituals that had to be observed concerning what food could be eaten by whom and when. For instance, among the Kirimojong, the meat from cows and goats was eaten only if they died— they were not killed for food. The Bambuti obtained most of their food by hunting, and they were very skilled at it. Among the Bagwe, women were not allowed to eat lung fish, chicken, and eggs, while among the Banyoro, certain foods were reserved for particular functions, such as guest meals, which always consisted of millet and meat. Potatoes were never given to guests, except in times of scarcity, and in times of real scarcity, the Bahima could just subsist on milk and blood.

Among the Iteso, the men did not eat with women, but ate separately seated on stools, tree stumps, or stones. The women sat on mats in a circle around the food. Among the Basamia, Bagwe, and Banyole, women and girls ate together from the same plate, while boys and their fathers would also eat together. Unnecessary talking was not allowed at mealtimes.

In poor Ugandan homes the cook's aim is to provide as filling a meal as possible. Meat is expensive so starchy foods, such as potatoes, cassava, and millet are used generously. If meat is served at all, it is used sparingly to give some flavor to the other ingredients.

A SOCIAL OCCASION

Food is very important at social gatherings, and Ugandans will find any excuse to feast on good food. Communal eating is still held in high regard so families and friends gather and eat together mainly in homes. A relative or friend visiting after a long absence can expect celebrations with music and dancing as well as a table laden with food. On such occasions the food is rarely elaborate, but there is lots of it, and it is prepared with care. Other important occasions, such as festivals, christenings, holidays, birthdays, and anniversaries, all warrant a big celebratory feast for family and friends.

WATER SUPPLY

The adequate supply of fresh, safe water to Ugandan villages and homesteads is an ongoing problem. Poor water quality has disastrous consequences. Stagnant water causes disease to spread rapidly within small communities and can endanger lives, especially those of young children, causing fatal disease.

Public awareness of the dangers of unclean water is growing, and the people living in rural Ugandan villages understand the need for an improvement in the standard of the water they have been using in the past. In the past, if the nearest freshwater supply was a few miles away, women would make the trip in an attempt to protect themselves and their children from disease. This chore would be repeated daily, in order to feed the demands of the family. In many towns and villages today this is seldom necessary as most villages have one or more wells with a constant supply of clean, fresh water.

Projects have been set up by charities worldwide to supply expert manpower, in the form of engineers and geologists, and funding to build these freshwater wells throughout the country.

COOKING FOR THE MASSES

In the less sophisticated Ugandan kitchens, food is often prepared in large batches and quantities sufficient to feed a large extended family, or several smaller families within one community. The staples of potatoes, cassava, matoke, and beans form the basis of most main meals and can be cooked slowly well ahead of time and left simmering while the family is out working.

There is little variety in the daily menu prepared in a Ugandan kitchen—breakfast, lunch, and the evening meal often closely resemble one another. The selection depends on what is available at the market or what fish or meat the male family members have been able to catch that day.

Babies are introduced to solid foods at an early age, and soft foods such as boiled matoke and cassava mashed up with milk and sugarcane juice provide a balance of healthy nutrients.

Above: **A boy prepares a huge pot of boiled matoke for his family.**

Opposite: **A modern water pump supplying fresh water to a village.**

Matoke is the staple diet of Ugandans living in the south. In the north matoke is less common where millet, sorghum, cornmeal, and cassava are favored.

MATOKE

Matoke is Uganda's national food and one of the oldest dishes in the world. It is popular in many parts of Uganda and is grown in almost every homestead in Buganda. When the matoke fruit is ready, the leaves are cut off and kept for cooking, together with the plant fibers, which are used to tie the leaves together during cooking. The stalks are put in the saucepan too, together with the leaves, to ease the steaming process.

To cook matoke:

Peel off the green skin of the matoke fruit. Place the white flesh in the leaves and tie up with leaf fibers.

Put the banana stalk, some ribs from the leaves, and the leaves into the bottom of a large saucepan containing more leaves. Steam for about one hour. Then remove the bundle and mold the matoke, while still inside the leaves.

Put it back in the saucepan and onto the fire to enhance the flavor. When the matoke is ready it will turn yellow. Matoke can be eaten with many sauces, stews, curries, and other vegetables.

DRINKS

Other than milk and water, which is now obtained quite easily in many villages, most tribes brewed some form of beer that they drank with their meals. The Baganda made a beer from bananas called *mwenge bigere* ("m-wen-GAY bee-GER-ay") which was alcoholic, and another non-alcoholic type called *omubisi* ("om-oo-BEE-see"). The Bakiga made an alcoholic beer from sorghum called *omuranba* ("om-oo-RAN-ba"), while the Bahutu called their sorghum-based beer *amarwa* ("ah-MAR-wa"). Different types of beer are still a popular drink in Uganda today.

Nonalcoholic carbonated drinks imported from the West are available, but more popular are the local, cheaper alternatives.

Uganda Breweries supplies beer and lagers throughout Uganda, as well as to other East African nations.

The success of a
particular crop,
and the diet of a
family community,
is dependent on
rainfall and the
length of the dry
season. Areas with
a low annual
rainfall are
limited to growing
sorghum, millet,
and cassava. In
areas where the
dry season lasts
from five to seven
months, the
problem is more
serious. Farmers
must either move
their family
homestead to an
area with fertile
soil, or walk for
miles to the
nearest suitable
plot of land.

OLUWOMBO

Oluwombo ("o-loo-WOM-bo") is a delicious Kiganda dish introduced during the reign of Kabaka Mwanga in 1887 by his chief cook, Kawunta. It is an important dish among the Baganda and used to be served to important state visitors, to the kabaka, and other Baganda chiefs. It is a form of stew made from chicken, goat, pork, beef, or even groundnuts mixed with mushrooms.

The traditional way to make *oluwombo* is to take a newly unwrapped banana leaf or leaves from a banana tree and remove the middle vein. Hold the leaves over a fire of burning banana peel. The smoke bleaches the leaves and gives them a smoky flavor. The "cooked" leaves should be folded carefully to avoid cracking them so that they will hold the ingredients of the *oluwombo*.

Make the *oluwombo* stew using smoked chicken pieces, pork, beef, tomatoes, or nuts. Place the *oluwombo* in the leaves with some salt and a little water. Take a large saucepan and pack it with more chopped banana, banana stalks, banana leaves, and some water.

Place the prepared *oluwombo* inside and cover with more banana leaves. Place the saucepan over a fire and cook for approximately one hour, and serve hot.

To make *oluwombo* without banana leaves:

Oluwombo can also be prepared using foil as a substitute (you may need to use more than one layer) for banana leaves. Cook a beef roast in the oven until cooked, but still tender. Place the beef on the foil.

Add seasonings to the meat, then some chopped onions, tomatoes, and other vegetables that might be used to prepare a beef stew, such as carrots, zuccini, eggplant, or mushrooms.

Add a small amount of water.

Wrap all the ingredients carefully in the tin foil and place in a large casserole dish.

Cook in the oven on a very low setting for 3–4 hours, until the flavor of the vegetables has been sealed into the meat. Serve hot the traditional Ugandan way—in a large pot placed in the center of the table.

FRUITS AND VEGETABLES

There is a vast array of tropical fruits available in Uganda, thanks to the lush vegetation growing high in the mountains throughout the country. Markets are held in most villages at least once a week, and sometimes every day. Local women gather there to make their selection from the range of fresh produce on display. It is a social event, as much as a domestic necessity, and provides an opportunity for social interaction with neighbors.

Tomatoes, avocados, citrus fruits, matoke, and many different root vegetables all form part of a healthy, balanced diet. Traditionally, rural tribes living in the savannas of Uganda based their diet solely on meat. Today, however, an improved transportation and communications system means that every market has access to a supply of fresh fruits and vegetables.

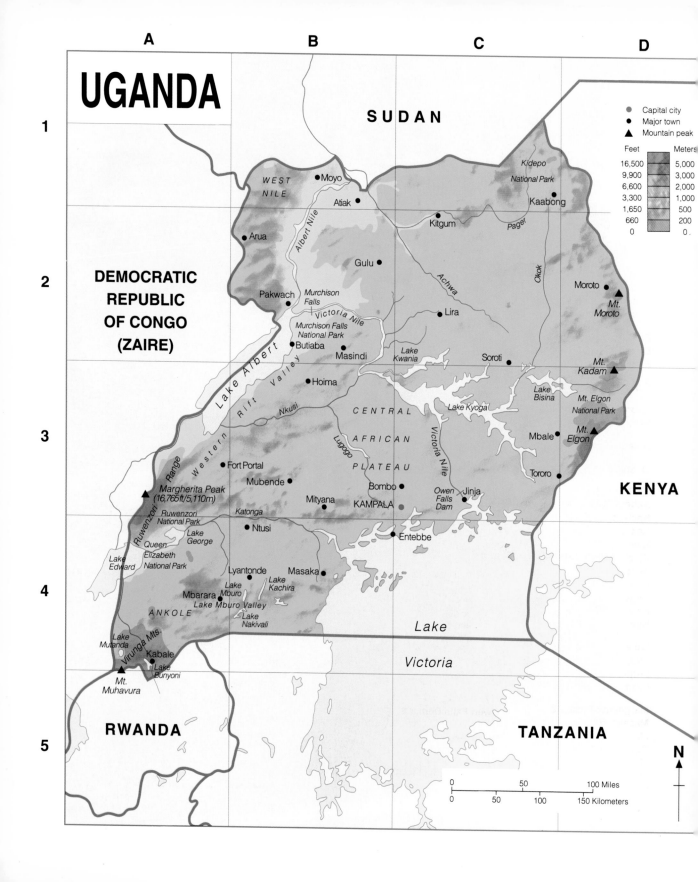

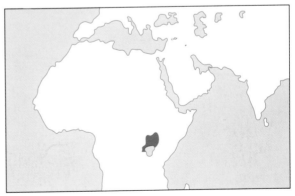

QUICK NOTES

OFFICIAL NAME
Republic of Uganda

AREA
93,070 square miles
(241,040 square km)

POPULATION
20.8 million (1997 estimate)

CAPITAL
Kampala

OFFICIAL LANGUAGES
English and Kiswahili

HIGHEST POINT
Margherita Peak (16,765 ft / 5,110 m)

LARGEST LAKE
Lake Victoria

MAIN ETHNIC GROUPS
Bantu, Nilo Hamites, Luo

MAIN RELIGIONS
Christianity, traditional African beliefs, Hinduism, Islam

RIVERS
Nile, Albert Nile, Victoria Nile

CLIMATE
Tropical, with low rainfall in the west

MAJOR CITIES
Kampala, Entebbe, Jinja, Mbale, Gulu

REGIONS
Northwestern Region, Northern Region, Northeastern Region, Western Region, Eastern Region, Southern Region, Central Region

NATIONAL FLAG
Black, yellow and red stripes that run horizontally and are repeated in the same order. Crested crane in the middle that symbolizes the national emblem

CURRENCY
Uganda shilling
US$1 = 1,000 shillings

MAIN EXPORTS
Coffee, corn, beans, fish products, gold

MAJOR IMPORTS
Machinery and transportation equipment

POLITICAL LEADERS
Yoweri Kaguta Museveni—president since 1986
Milton Obote—president from 1962 to 1971
Idi Amin Dada—president from 1971 to 1978

ANNIVERSARIES
Liberation Day (January 26)
National Independence Day (October 9)

GLOSSARY

abasomi ("ah-ba-SO-mee")
New converts to Christianity.

Abayudaya
Small isolated community of Ugandan Jews.

baami ("BAA-mee")
Bagandan chiefs.

bakopi ("BA-koh-pee")
Serfs in Bagandan society.

balangira ("BA-lan-gee-ra")
Bagandan princes.

balubaale ("BA-loo-ba-lay")
Ghosts of the dead believed by the Baganda to live in the form of mythical tribal figures.

homestead
A self-sufficient rural home with a plot of land to keep animals and grow crops.

indaro ("in-DA-ro")
Religious shrine of the Basamia and Bagwe.

kabaka ("ka-BA-ka")
Tribal king.

kanzu ("KAN-zoo")
Bagandan traditional attire.

misambwa ("mi-SAM-bwa")
Spirits of the dead living in the form of natural objects, such as trees or stones.

mizimu ("mi-ZEE-moo")
Ghosts of the dead believed by the Baganda to haunt living enemies of the dead person.

nalinya ("na-LEEN-ya")
Royal sister.

namasole ("NA-ma-so-lay")
Queen mother.

nankasa ("nan-KA-sa")
A popular Bagandan ceremonial dance.

okwabya olumbe ("ok-wa-by-YA o-LOOM-bay")
Funeral rites.

okwalula abaana ("ok-wa-loo-LA ah-BA-na")
Ceremony in which children are given clan names.

okwanjula ("ok-wan-JOO-la")
Formal introduction of the husband before an arranged marriage.

oluwombo ("o-loo-WOM-bo")
Bagandan stew served to important state visitors.

rwot ("RWOT")
Hereditary ruler in the Acholi tribe.

sorghum
Tropical grass plant which produces grain, forage, and syrup.

BIBLIOGRAPHY

Blauer, Ettagale. *Uganda: Enchantment of the World*. Danbury, Connecticut: Children's Press, 1997.

Briggs, Philip. *Uganda (3rd ed)*. Chalfont St. Peter, England: Bradt Publishing, 1999.

Creed, Alexander. *Uganda (Major World Nations)*. Broomall, Pennsylvania: Chelsea House Publishers, 1998.

Hodd, Michael. *East Africa Handbook: with Kenya, Tanzania, Uganda and Ethiopia (5th ed)*. Chicago, Illinois: Passport Books, 1998.

Measures, Bob. *Amin's Uganda*. London: Minerva Press, 1998.

Ofcansky, Thomas. *Uganda: Tarnished Pearl of Africa (Nations of the Modern World, Africa)*. Oxford, England: Westview Press, 1996.

INDEX

INDEX

INDEX

PICTURE CREDITS
Camera Press: 32, 35, 62, 74, 79
John Denham: 5, 10, 28, 29, 39, 58, 101,
  109, 114
Hutchison Library: 17, 26, 34, 40, 43, 54,
  56, 81, 86, 87, 94, 103, 107, 123
Images of Africa: 11, 12, 14, 15 (top), 38,
  47, 53, 59, 67, 70, 76, 90, 95, 118, 121
Paul Joynson-Hicks/Laure Communica-
  tions: 1, 7, 13, 15 (bottom), 36, 37, 64,
  88, 93, 104, 119
Jason Laure: 18, 48, 83, 85, 89, 105, 111
Eric Miller/iAfrika: 73
Liba Taylor: 4, 80, 108, 117
North Wind Picture Archives: 20, 22
Sue O'Connor/Christine Osborne Pictures: 3
Christine Osborne Pictures: 25
Still Pictures: 49, 52, 98, 113
Topham Picturepoint: 6, 16, 24, 31, 78,
  106
Trip Photographic Library: 9, 19, 23, 30,
  33, 41, 44, 45, 46, 50, 51, 55, 57, 60, 61,
  66, 68, 71, 72, 77, 82, 84, 91, 92, 96, 97,
  99, 100, 110, 112, 116

ADDITIONAL RESEARCH
Sarah Kafeero